Voices of the
Fourth Generation

Voices of the
Fourth Generation
China's Poets Today

An Anthology

Edited, with an Introduction and Notes by
Keming Liu

Floating World Editions

First edition, 2010

Published by Floating World Editions, Inc., 26 Jack Corner Road, Warren, CT 06777. Protected by copyright under the terms of the International Copyright Union; all rights reserved. Except for fair use in book reviews, no part of this book may be reproduced for any reason by any means, including any method of photographic reproduction, without the permission of the publisher.

Printed in the United States

ISBN 978-1-891640-58-2

Library of Congress Cataloging-in-Publication data available

Jacket front shows *Memories (Me)*, by Sheng Qi, courtesy of the International Center of Photography, by permission of the artist; jacket back shows *Dialogue*, by Zhang Da-li, courtesy of the artist and CourtYard Gallery.

To honor the memory of my mother, Li Shu-ying, who gave me my childhood education by candlelight during the early days of the Cultural Revolution, when schools were shut and books burned. I wish she could be here to harvest the fruit of the seeds she planted long ago. She lives in the hearts of her children and her students.

献给母亲

李淑英。感谢母亲在我童年期间给予的良好的家庭环境及循循教导。在动荡不安的文革时期，母亲正直的品格，坚定了我走向人生的步伐。在天之灵的母亲一定会看到，您曾培育的树苗，如今已是枝繁叶茂，喜结硕果。

母亲，您永远活在您儿女的心中。

Contents

The Artists

Biographical Sketches

Acknowledgments

Special thanks are due to the PSC-CUNY Research Foundation and the Diversity Committee of the City University of New York for continuously providing generous support, without which this volume could not have been completed. Thanks are also due to the late Dr. Tom Tam, a gentleman, scholar and stalwart advocate of Asian intellectuals in New York, who quietly supported my scholarship and guided me in my career. This volume is a collaboration among the distinguished editorial and design professionals of Floating Worlds Editions, a renowned publisher of Asian art and literary titles, particularly publisher and editor Ray Furse, whose advice, vision, and commitment to the project have been invaluable, and designer Liz Trovato, who worked tirelessly to produce the elegant look of the book. My heartfelt thanks are also extended to Shao Ning-zhi (邵宁之), Yuan Jia-li (苑佳丽) and their daughter Peanuts (花生) for their efforts in tracking down sources and providing invaluable advice and understanding of the new China that I left behind some two decades ago. I am also grateful to the cover artist, Sheng Qi (盛奇), now an international art star, who generously granted permission to use the powerful and personal masterpiece which graces the cover. These pages would be empty without the collaboration of the poets whose unconditional support for this project made it all possible. I wish to thank my colleague and poet, Linda Jackson, for her encouragement and expert advice during this project. Without my dear college classmates and friends, Lou Mei-ying (娄梅婴) and Ren Guo-qing (任国庆), and their candid critique of my rough drafts and their scholarly encouragement, the project would be missing valuable elements. I especially wish to thank my family on both sides of the Pacific: my brother, Liu Ke-qiang (刘克强), for his efforts researching and answering my queries in Chinese and his unconditional love; my husband, Charles Riley, for his continuous support and time spent reading early drafts and making helpful suggestions.

—Keming Liu
Cutchogue, New York
August 2009

Sources

Grateful acknowledgment is made to the following for permission to include the poems and art in this anthology:

Duo Yu

"Ode to the West Wind" (93) from *Contemporary Poetry*, © Lijiang Publishers, 2004–2005. Reprinted by permission of Lijiang Publishers.

Ge Mai

"Jade Clothes with Golden Inlay" (6) from *The Complete Poetic Works of Ge Mai*, © SDXjoint Publishing Company, 1999. Reprinted by permission of SDXjoint Publishing Company.

Hai Zi

"Overlooking the Ocean in the Warm and Flowering Spring" (4) from *Selected Poems of Contemporary Chinese Poets*, © Hebei Educational Press, 2004. Reprinted by permission of Hebei Educational Press.

Hu Xu-dong

"Snowy Night" (53) from *Tomorrow*, © Hunan Literature and Art Publishing House, 2003. Reprinted by permission of Hunan Literature and Art Publishing House.

Hu Zi-bo

"Relieved" (76) and "Crossroads" (78) from *Contemporary Poetry*, © Lijiang Publishers, 2004–2005. Reprinted by permission of Lijiang Publishers.

Huang Jin-ming

"Old Hutong Lament" (69) from *Heading Into Thin Air*, © Beijing Relay Press, 1997. Reprinted by permission of Beijing Relay Press.

Jiang Fei

"The Roofer" (55) and "The Woodsman" (58) from *Selected Poems of Contemporary Chinese Poets*, © Hebei Educational Press, 2004. Reprinted by permission of Hebei Educational Press.

"The Prickly Pepper Tree" (60) from *Solo Drama*, © South China Press, 2009. Reprinted by permission of South China Press.

Liu Chun

"Purity" (46) and "An Earthly Morning" (48) from *Tomorrow*, © Hunan Literature and Art Publishing House, 2003. Reprinted by permission of Hunan Literature and Art Publishing House.

Xie Xiang-nan

"Report of a Work-related Injury" (79) from *Contemporary Poetry*, © Lijiang
   Publishers, 2004–2005. Reprinted by permission of Lijiang Publishers.

Yang Chun-min

"Distant Relatives" (63) from *Selected Poems of Contemporary Chinese Poets*,
   © Hebei Educational Press, 2004. Reprinted by permission of Hebei
   Educational Press.

Yin Li-chuan

"Hidden" (20), "Old Zhang, the Retiree" (23), "Mother" (27), "Vase"
   (34), and "Cause and Effect" (36) from *Tomorrow*, © Hunan Literature
   and Art Publishing House, 2003. Reprinted by permission of Hunan
   Literature and Art Publishing House.

"The Old Woman" (22), "City Thief" (25), "Orange" (28), "Lover" (29),
   "Passing by the Workers" (30), "Hand" (31) and "Chinese Rap" (33) from
   Contemporary Poetry, © Lijiang Publishers, 2004–2005. Reprinted by
   permission of Lijiang Publishers.

"Remembering New Zealand" (35) from Selected Poems of *Contemporary
   Chinese Poets*, © Hebei Educational Press, 2004. Reprinted by permission
   of Hebei Educational Press.

Yu Xiang

"The Sun Shines Where It Needs To" (41), "Just Thinking That" (43), and "2002,
   I Have" (44) from *Tomorrow*, © Hunan Literature and Art Publishing House,
   2003. Reprinted by permission of Hunan Literature and Art Publishing House.

Zhu Qing-he

"After the Rain" (50) and "The Grape Seller" (51) from *Tomorrow*, © Hunan
   Literature and Art Publishing House, 2003. Reprinted by permission of
   Hunan Literature and Art Publishing House.

Illustration credits: Cao Fei, *Beautiful Dog Brows* (118), courtesy of *Elle*, by the
   artist; Cao Fei, *Not Going Home Tonight* (119), © Cao Fei, by permission of
   the artist; Zhang Da-li, *Demolition; World Financial Center, Beijing; Demoli-
   tion: Forbidden City, Beijing*; and *Dialogue*, courtesy of 367Art, Inc., and
   the CourtYard Gallery, Beijing, by permission of the artist; Leong Sze-tsung,
   Old Fengdu and *No. 6 Huashishang Fourth Lane*, courtesy of the International
   Center of Photography and Asia Society, by permission of the artist; Sheng
   Qi, *Memories (Me)* (103 and jacket), courtesy of the International Center of
   Photography, by permission of the artist.

Introduction
The Post-Confucian Poetics of China

"...and what are poets for in a destitute time?"

—Johann Christian Friedrich Hölderlin,
Brot Und Wein (*Bread and Wine*)

Destitute is not a word likely to be used in any description of China today, with its stratospheric growth threatening to dominate the world economic order. Certainly the adjectives that apply to a success story of this magnitude would all seem to be antonyms of "destitute," and most of the coverage devoted to the boom is replete with one hyperbole after another for the new prosperity. Yet material comfort was also the hallmark of the era that the German poet Hölderlin characterized as destitute, a period when he perceived that Europe was suffering from a decline that had nothing to do with its burgeoning economies. In his view, night had fallen after Herakles, Dionysos, and Christ had left the world. A bleak echo of his anxiety has crept into the poetry and art being made in the fastest-growing nation of our own time. It poses a question that offers a new variant on Hölderlin's timeless warning: Has Confucius left China?

The Chinese poetry presented here, work of the movement called the Fourth Generation, can be more easily defined by a time frame (the last decade of the twentieth century) than a zeitgeist. The young poets gathered in these pages grew up after the Cultural Revolution (1966–76), attended college after the Tian'anmen Square uprising (1989) and some now hold prominent positions in publishing or academia. To begin to understand the meaning and importance of Fourth Generation poetry, a glimpse of its predecessors is necessary. It is also important to track the uneasy relationship between politics and literature in China's turbulent twentieth century.

Modern Chinese literature is generally considered to have begun with Lu Xun (鲁迅, 1881–1936), a leading figure of the May Fourth era (from May 4, 1919, through the 1920s). His masterful short story, "A Madman's Diary," appeared in 1918 and set off a modern literary style that is still echoed in the works of writers today. Lu Xun, who trained as a medical doctor, marked a sharp break with China's literary tradition, attacking Confucianism, initiating a vernacular style of writing, and promoting scientific thinking. The writers who took up his ideas were labeled the First Generation, and included such revered names as Lao She (老舍, 1899–1966), Shen Cong-wen (沈从文, 1902–88), Xiao Hong (萧红, 1911–42), and many more. Their voices reflected a renewed look at China's social, political, and historical conditions. For thousands of years, the nation's literati labored with the entrenched conviction that China was the Middle Kingdom. That tenet released its grip with the works of the First Generation, when direct challenges were launched against the feudal system. It was a time when literature and ideology were moving lockstep together, as poets, novelists, and story writers echoed the basic beliefs of Communism.

Politics played a dramatically different role in defining the next movement. Emboldened by Chairman Deng Xiaoping's call for an "emancipation of thought" in 1979, the Second Generation nonetheless felt forced to disguise itself behind the sobriquet of Menglong (Misty). The social turmoil and political persecution of dissidents of the Second Generation led to a fallow period in China's literary scene by the end of the twentieth century. It was not until after the Cultural Revolution that the Second Generation of prominent literary figures emerged with leading figures such as Bei Dao (北岛, 1949–) and Gu Cheng (顾城, 1956–93), who spearheaded a New Age poetic expression that stresses the self not as part of a social collective consciousness but in the spirit of individual sanctity. The coverage of Chinese poetic evolution stops just about this point in most, if not all, Western literary anthologies, and little has been written about the Third Generation of the late 1980s except for a few journal articles, notably Michelle Yeh's essay on "The Cult of Poetry."[1]

This anthology aims to redress that oversight, introducing for the first time in one volume the most significant new voices to a global audience. In an age of cyber-literature, print defers to online dissemination. In the late 1980s, the Third Generation of Chinese poets started appearing in online chat-rooms where poets receive instantaneous response and criticism from a wide-ranging readership. The leading figures of this school are Xiao An (小安, 1964–), Hai Zi (海子, 1964–1989), Yang Li (杨黎, 1962–), He Xiao-zhu (何小竹, 1963–), and Ji Mu Lang Ge (吉木狼格, 1963–) among others. This *soi-disant* "Fei-Fei" School of Dadaistic poets, born in the 1960s, chose narrative as a compositional strat-

---

1. Michelle Yeh, "The 'Cult of Poetry' in Contemporary China." *The Journal of Asian Studies* 55. 1 (February 1996): 51 – 80.

egy to anchor a particular relationship between man and his position in society. They reflect on their existence as the "lucky" generation by contrast with their predecessors who suffered during the Cultural Revolution. In the face of China's transformation, however, the Third Generation enjoys a less than prominent social position. Their hopes were torpedoed by their zeal for political change after the nearly successful 1989 student protests and subsequent oppression by the government. As Chinese culture turned its back on politics to grasp new wealth, their dissident voices were left even further behind. Xiao An's "Flight," for example, features a young horse whose desire to join its older siblings symbolizes the Third Generation's feeling of inadequacy in failing to foster change. Does the colt intend to catch up with the herd or flee to some solitary equine utopia?

"Flight" (飞奔)

There's a pony
contemplating a canter—
the way the other horses run
to a grassy place and
eat a delicious lunch.

But forget about it.
He's just a little colt
too little, too young.
Galloping
is merely contemplation.

一匹马
他想奔跑
象令一匹马的样子
跑到青草多的地方
吃上一顿美味的午餐

可是不行啊
他只是一匹小马
太小太小的
飞奔的感觉
在心里想想罢了

The Third Generation's disillusionment and, to a large extent, failure, resulted in a wave of suicides in the early 1990s. The ideal state they envisioned constantly clashed with the demolition of the traditional legacies they romanticized in their verse. The rapid disappearance of China's history dealt an indelible blow to the fragile mindset of these neo-romantics who, like Henry David Thoreau, longed for that Walden of pastoral and ascetic idealism. A particularly Thoreauvian note is struck by Hai Zi:

"Overlooking the Ocean in the Warm and Flowering Spring"
(面朝大海，春暖花开)

> Starting tomorrow, I'm going to be happy-go-lucky,
> feed the horses, chop the wood, travel the world
> Starting tomorrow, I'll be sure to eat well, plenty of
> vegetables.
> I'll have a shack overlooking the ocean, in the warm and
> flowering spring
>
> Starting tomorrow, I'll write to every member of my family
> I'll tell them that I've been struck
> by the lightning of happiness.
> I'll tell each one of them
>
> Give every river every mountain
> a cozy name
> Stranger, I wish you the best, too
> I wish you a brilliant future
> I wish you a faithful lover
> I wish you happiness on earth
> Me, I just want a view of the ocean
> in the warm and flowering spring

从明天起，做一个幸福的人
喂马，劈柴，周游世界
从明天起，关心粮食和蔬菜
我有一所房子，面朝大海，春暖花开

从明天起，和每一个亲人通信
告诉他们我的幸福
那幸福的闪电告诉我的
我将告诉每一个人

给每一条河每一座山取一个温暖的名字
陌生人，我也为你祝福
愿你有一个灿烂的前程
愿你有情人终成眷属
愿你在尘世获得幸福
我只愿面朝大海，春暖花开

Behind the beneficent disguise of a hermit longing for tranquil solitude hides the urgent desire to abandon the material world, which is buzzing with the zest for money but slowly losing its moral grip. It is no coincidence that "Overlooking the Ocean" confirms a clear asceticism in Hai Zi's philosophical outlook. By Hai Zi's body on that portentous day of his suicide on March 26, 1989, was a bag filled with four books: *The Bible*, Thoreau's *Walden*, Thor Heyerdahl's *Kon Tiki*, and Joseph Conrad's *Selected Stories*. Notably, three of the four books explore the epic wilderness adventures of a solitary man, a dominant theme in Hai Zi's poetry. A child protégé, Hai Zi was born into a peasant family in Anhui province who gave him the name Zha Hai-sheng, literally "sea-born," which was transformed into his pen-name Hai Zi, "son of the sea." He passed the national entrance examination to enter the prestigious Beijing University at age 15 in 1978. At the time of his death, he was living as a recluse in a sparse two-room concrete apartment in Changping, an outlying mountainous district about twenty-five miles northwest of Beijing. Lined with floor-to-ceiling bookshelves, the apartment contained no TV or computer, not even a radio. Hai Zi shut himself off from the world to find inner peace and a meaningful existence. Using suicide as a means of self-expression, this martyr to literary idealism remains a prominent representative of the Third Generation poets. He fell victim to the same strong desire to assert his identity that intricately entwined his predecessors, whose work is never free of moral implications. His legacy inspired millions of fans, some of whom became the nucleus of today's Fourth Generation poets. Among them is Ge Mai, whose adoration of Hai Zi not only left him despondent but prompted an outpouring of fine poems of acclaim. Sadly, Ge Mai followed Hai Zi's footsteps, ending his life in 1991, when he was only twenty-four years old. Before his death, Ge Mai eulogized Hai Zi in numerous essays and poems, in which he invoked the imagery of the "son of the sea" and the spring season full of flowers, a running metaphor in Chinese literature for hope, as in this lyric:

"Jade Clothes with Golden Inlay" (金缕玉衣)

> Seeing your undying morning glory, torrents of tears fill me
> summer burning, autumn drunk
> but I shall be gone
> to the darkest corner of all times
> content, I lift my eyes but see no future
> I shall sink to the depth of the sea
> great waves, cool autumn breeze
>
> I shall be the youngest among the dead
> but not in the least the best
> I will not embrace thousands of children on the throne of hell
> but I shall be the volcano of hell
> looking back to a short life and long regret
> I shall become a stag or pretend to be one
> repeating lies a thousand times until they become truth
> I shall become a tree straight up into the sky
>
> You shall take my shining skeleton
> like a sleeping baby in the sea's embrace
> like the village surrounded by flowers
> Spring, your blue water is my long-cherished wish
> my old and ailing life like a candle guttering in the wind

今日，看到你不灭的青光，我浊泪涟涟
夏日如烧，秋日如醉
而我将故去
将退踞到世间最黑暗的年代
固步自封，举目无望
我将沉入那最深的海底
波涛阵阵，秋风送爽

我将成为众尸之中最年轻的一个
但不会是众尸之王
不会在地狱的王位上怀抱上前的儿女
我将成为地狱的火山
回忆着短暂的一生和漫长的遗憾
我将成为鹿，或指鹿为马
将谎话重复千遍，变作真理
我将成为树木，直插苍穹

而你将怀抱我光辉的骨骼
像大海怀抱熟睡的婴孩
花朵怀抱村庄
是春天，沧浪之水，是夙愿
是我的风烛残年

Poetry as a long-established tradition in Chinese literature experienced a massive revival in the twenty-first century, ironically under similar conditions to the Tang and Song milieu, a golden period in the arts when China enjoyed strikingly similar prosperity and influence. Unlike the elitist Tang and Song lyrics, Fourth Generation poetry appeals to the general reader with a consciously anti-pedantic style. The breakthrough of the Fourth Generation poets lies in their jettisoning of an obvious desire to change the world around them. They no longer believe they can or should speak for their generation. Disengaging from the *isms* that had come into fashion during the 1980s, the Fourth Generation made a conscious choice in their linguistic representation of concepts and events to stay away from laborious judgments of good and evil, implied or otherwise. Like the

Third Generation, the Fourth Generation poets of the late 1990s found their platform on the internet. Daily postings of newly minted poetry received instant praise or criticism, spawning voluminous traffic on the poets' blogs.

Defying the influences of the Second and the Third Generation, the Fourth Generation reflects an emerging reliance on individualism, soul searching, and reflection. It tends, however, toward fashioning a "couldn't-care-less" attitude. Rebelling against China's scholastic and folkloric traditions and the collective drive for economic gain and financial well being, the Fourth Generation poets are the Generation Y who grew up with MTV and hip-hop.[2] They are less concerned with far-fetched romanticism than with everyday existence. The selves they pursue are their own realistic identities within an ever-changing China, where money talks. They are aware of the fact that poetry does not make a dent in the national craze for profit, nor does it earn them the status accorded to high-tech millionaires and movie stars. Yet, they choose to engage in poetry, projecting a rare and pure Heideggerian individualism befitting an era when a whole way of life is disappearing and being replaced overnight by another. The influx of Western culture and aesthetic appreciation inspired a voracious appetite that was almost entirely unknown in China until the 1980s. The highly complex philosophies of Descartes and Kant were made unlikely best sellers on the Chinese literary market together with translations of T.S. Eliot, Hölderlin, Rilke, W.H. Auden, and Franz Kafka. Allusions to Auden can be found in Yang Chun-min's (杨春民, 1979–)"Distant Relatives," in which the poet directly quoted Auden's "Sonnets from China" as a lead to the portrayal of a distant relative who cut his finger to avoid being drafted into the army during the war.[3] While Yin Li-chuan's (尹丽川, 1973–) "Vase" invokes imagery from T.S. Eliot's "Four Quartets,"[4] Shi Yi-long's (石一龙) "Empty

---

2. In ancient China, only those who had received elite education and mastered the complicated linguistic system could become writers. "Mandarin" became the Western term for these politically empowered members of the intelligentsia. When the Communists gained power in 1949, they imitated the Soviet ideological and cultural system. The government took care of all the "writers" who obeyed the national ideology, paid their salaries, and offered them health care and travel privileges. The Writers' Association became a massive government bureaucracy, and the system became an important component of the planned economy. Under these circumstances, a writer had to become a member of the official Writers' Association before his or her work could appear in literary journals and anthologies.

3. W.H. Auden, "Sonnets from China, XIII." W.H. Auden Collected Poems. Ed. Edward Mendelson. New York: Random House, 1976: 154.

4. T.S. Eliot, "Four Quartets." The Complete Poems and Plays of T.S. Eliot 1909–1950. New York: Harcourt, Brace & World, Inc., 1971: 115–122.

Fortress" comments on Kafka. Alongside these volumes were others by contemporary Western poets such as Allen Ginsberg and collections of hip-hop lyrics. Internal change and external influence converged to give rise to a hybrid aesthetic philosophy that the Fourth Generation poets embraced. It forced an utterly new kind of artistic encounter among poets who reassessed China's extraordinarily rich cultural tradition with an eye to determining how to present a viable poetics for the present. The Fourth Generation voices ostensibly profess a new kind of rationality. They worry less about conforming to the theory of knowledge provided by common social practices. Rather, they constitute their own epistemically based knowledge, distant from the opinions of others. It embodies the Cartesian principle of "*dubito, cogito, ergo sum,*" with special emphasis upon the doubt. They depart from the views of such philosophers as Ludwig Wittgenstein, Lev Vygotsky, and Michel Foucault, who held that rationality is construed by social practices. Like the New York School of poets who challenged the norm, only three decades later the Fourth Generation poets on the other side of the globe also came to appreciate the view that acceptance is not necessarily a blessing, nor rejection a curse.

Western influence is clearly evident in their composition as well as technique. Passion and romanticism are no longer the driving motive. Instead, they veer toward narrating everyday, insignificant events and encounters, not sparing any effort in attending to details. They adopt Philip Larkin's attraction to the mundane, clearly and unmistakably pronounced in an essay published in *The Listener* in 1968 and widely circulated in China. "When I came to Hardy it was with the sense of relief that I didn't have to jack myself up to a concept of poetry that lay outside my own life … One could simply relapse back into one's own life and write from it."[5] For Fourth Generation poets, this stance is not a rhetorical end but a hermeneutic strategy. Their work deliberately constructs ideas as, in the Heideggerian sense, "objects-in-the-world." In Yin Li-chuan's (尹丽川) "This Must Have Been Well-Planned," the speaker's personal life is juxtaposed with outside events. None seems to make a significant impression on her consciousness. It is as if each event is a part on an ironic assembly line where workers mechanically handle their individual responsibilities, in isolation. Upon examination, however, one discerns a cognitive pattern rich in imagery: The

---

5. Philip Larkin, "Philip Larkin Praises the Poetry of Thomas Hardy." *The Listener,* 25 July 1968:111.

Iraq war is alluded to in the line about Saddam's disappearance; sickness is invoked by SARS; bodily pain is caused by the lovers' separation; and the wilderness is brought into the drama by the bareness of the wintry Himalayas. In the scholar Patrick Hogan's words, "An image is likely to prime associated ideas and memories... It is likely to make those ideas and memories more accessible to active cognitive processing, thus more consequential for our understanding of the work and our response to it."[6] The timely mortal images of the Iraq war and SARS invoke a parallel to the stomach pains signaling the death of a romantic relationship. Although the poet's voice seems stoic, cold and numb on the surface, the images suggest the deep loss felt by the speaker/lover, articulating the unquestionable turmoil of emotional loss, social chaos, and natural disasters, and establishing a cogent correlation among the loose ends. She is not as "cool" as she pretends, and the reader's empathy adds emotional warmth.

"It Must Have Been Well-planned" (这一定是商量好的)

> After we parted
> Saddam vanished
> SARS broke out
> Nurses were braver than big sister
> My stomach still hurts.
> Frostbite got your leg
>   at the foot of the Himalayas,
> again, someone else climbed and claimed it
> They all said, "How great!"
>
> After we parted
> we never hugged again
> A young man was captured, beaten to death
> The assassins younger than you.

---

6. Patrick Hogan. "Literary Universals and Their Cultural Traditions: The Case of Poetic Imagery." *Consciousness, Literature and the Arts*, 6.2 (August 2005). Special Issue: Literary Universals.

我们分手以后
萨达姆突然失踪
SARS 借机出台
护士比姐姐更英勇
我仍旧胃疼
你在喜马拉雅山下冻伤了腿
喜马拉雅山又被人爬了
他们都说这很伟大

我们分手以后
再没有互相抱过
一个青年被人仓促打死
凶手们比你还年轻

(2003/05/06)

Yin's poem invokes China's industrialization and the commercialization of the late twentieth and early twenty-first centuries. The speaker's catatonic narration reflects a methodical gesture, signifying passive civil disobedience without much fanfare. The rich imagery, however, dominates Fourth Generation poetry and allows its words to delight us as we enter the China of the new era. An important correlative is offered by the visual arts. Like the poignant portrayal of the dehumanization of modern China's industrial revolution, Yin's

*Deda Chicken
Processing Plant.*
Photograph by
Edward Burtynsky
(courtesy of
Spoon).

poem echoes a dehumanization seen in photography by Edward Burtynsky, a Canadian who has been documenting China's development since the late 1990s. In *Deda Chicken Processing Plant*, each worker on the slaughterhouse assembly line resembles a dead chicken similar to the speaker in Yin's poem, emotionless and matter-of-fact.[7] Yet, Fourth Generation poets are all but detached. They actively participate in nightclub readings, online blogs, and enjoy full-time careers. They travel, read, and write, take in music and movies as people their age would. Writing poetry is another aspect of multitasking, used as an outlet for their innermost feelings. This burgeoning productivity of Chinese writers serves as a different index from the GDP to the growth of China's massive market force.

Poetry as a performance art in the dot-com era revived in nightclubs and teahouses, especially in the late 1990s. The oral tradition in China enjoys a long and illustrious history and has its roots in teahouse readings of *The Outlaws of the Marsh*, or *Journey to the West*, not unlike audio books in the West, except of course for the dramatic, kinetic, and ocular effects experienced in live reading. Along with the revival of teahouse readings of Chinese classics came chic poetry and hip-hop performances. Chinese poets of our time face competition over their share of the audience from both the "old" classic performance artists and the young, hip-hop singers. Condensed and sublime composition may elude an audience attuned to the instantaneous and fast-paced gratification of lower forms of media, so Fourth Generation poetry uses narrative to entertain. Poetry as a visual construct is not lost in the process. It becomes cool as space and form add to its auditory appeal.

Not since the fabled Tang and Song dynasties has China seen such an outburst of powerful poetry. Today's burgeoning talent has elevated poetry to a form of expression that has outstripped politics in its cultural vitality and importance. As their work grabbed the limelight, the poets diverged from the conservative, form-abiding precedent of past generations, even including the high Modernists of the early twentieth century. This anthology of the highlights of China's self-defined Fourth Generation serves not only to introduce the avant-garde of literati to the Western world, but also offers a glimpse into China's

---

7. *Spoon: The Taste of Contemporary Culture*, November/December 2005: 58.

modernization. Included in the anthology are voices from diverse walks of life. Some are poets by training while others are farmers, factory workers, engineers, and journalists. All are important constituents of China's brave new world of art and culture. This anthology is the first to bring to the attention of English-speaking readers a comprehensive and focused selection of contemporary Chinese poetry in translation since the June 4th massacre at Tiananmen Square in 1989.

With the move toward globalization, the Chinese government has resolutely attempted to eradicate any blemishes that may tarnish its reputation. It spent billions of dollars to build a modern capital in preparation for the 2008 Olympic Games. Old *hutongs* (lanes and courtyards) were replaced by glitzy, high voltage architecture designed by Rem Koolhaas (China Central Television's new complex), Paul Andreu (China's National Grand Theater), Jacques Herzog and Pierre de Meuron (the Olympic Stadium), and Riken Yamamoto (Jianwai SOHO, a commercial complex in Beijing). Millions of traditional homes were razed and residents relocated to high-rise apartments, forever destroying a communal cultural setting that is quintessentially Chinese. In response to the disappearance of such cultural relics, both visual and literary artists expressed their dismay. The West, recognizing China's booming cultural representation and its power in the global economy, responded powerfully to the new efflorescence of artistic expression. Starting in the summer of 2004, New York became the center of China heat with Robert Wilson's A-list Watermill Foundation party featuring six Chinese artists' work, "China Moon," and a joint exhibition by ICP and Asia Society headlined "Between Past and Future," featuring 130 works by 60 Chinese artists. A series of shows in New York and Florida spotlighted recent video works by the so-called Sixth Generation of filmmakers, whose work focuses on marginal, urban lives, as seen in films such as *Still Life* and *Unknown Pleasures* by Jia Zhangke (贾樟柯, 1970–) and *Beijing Bicycle* by Wang Xiaoshuai (王小帅, 1966–). This group followed a Fifth Generation of film makers that included Zhang Yimou (张艺谋, 1951–), director of *Raise the Red Lantern* (1991) and Chen Kaige, director of *Farewell, My Concubine* (1993), whose success had catapulted China back into the international film scene. To highlight China's artistic presence, MoMA, for the time in its history offered a retrospective of a Chinese film maker, Jia Zhangke (贾樟柯, 1970–), in September 2009, along with the Carnegie Hall program featuring the renowned composer Tan Dun (谭盾, 1957–) in October and November 2009, an all-Chinese festival celebrating its culture.

Like the cinematic and visual artists, though on a much quieter level that has not yet drawn a global audience, Chinese poets responded to the disappearing cultural traditions with the same dismay. These young poets differ from their immediate predecessors of the 1990s in two pronounced areas: social/economic consciousness and aesthetic appreciation. Fourth Generation poets are consciously aware of the reality that poetry does not earn them money or fame. They create art for art's sake, exploring personal worthiness against the backdrop of material wealth. The key discriminating element characterizing the Fourth Generation poets is that their view of individualism takes on the philosophy of existentialism while the Third Generation poets express the self as a cultural attitude. Due to this stress on the true sense of individualism, Fourth Generation poets exhibit a complex mix of self expression which a few poets' work cannot capture or command. Canvassing the group involves a wide range of themes and forms. One other feature of Fourth Generation poets is that they delve the linguistic extremes of style and poetic forms, taking advantage of the intricate relationship between language and society, using it as a tool to probe the engine of contemporary China as well as its history.

The aim of this project is to present an anthology of poetry that captures China's globalization in the past twenty years. Perhaps not all poems selected for this anthology are "masterpieces" by the standards of all critics. However, they are representative of the Chinese psyche of the moment. The selection has been made in order to provide a representative sample of the poetry appearing in the "boom" years when both capitalism and nationalism are rampant. The poems are taken from two official publications, *Zhongguo Dangdai Qingnian Shiren Shixuan* (Selected Poems of Contemporary Chinese Poets) and *Mingtian* (Tomorrow). Aside from myself as the sole editor and one of the translators, I have invited Joanna Sit, Jia-li Yuan, Jian-xun Zhao, and James Zhao to participate in translating the poems I selected. A brief biography is included for each translator.

In an effort to present a lucid and uniform volume, every effort has been made to weave the subtle emotional and psychological nuances of each poem with formal rigor in English translation. The forms run the gamut from metrical to free verse and prose narrative. Some are as brief as Haiku while others run a couple of pages long.

Most of the poems use political or social satire, as in "The Last Supper" by Ma Fei (马非, 1971–). Like other countries under totalitarian rule, such as Russia and Cuba, China has produced poets in a volatile time when the country is undergoing tremendous change both politically and economically. "The Last Supper" clearly alludes to the Biblical story, echoing a tradition in Chinese literary circles dating back to the early twentieth century when the first mass movement in modern Chinese history, the May Fourth Movement of 1919 prompted writers such as Lu Xun to write social satires heavily imbued with Western references. Like the poets selected for this anthology, the writers during that movement championed intellectual revolution and sociopolitical reform. "The Last Supper" represents a theme that recurs through the economic boom years. The descriptions of animals and insects are used to caricature individuals or social groups. The subtle implication of the chef's suggestion for dinner is exposed by the cat, who pipes up that human flesh should not be the choice as it is too bony. The political context for this includes a reference to the plight of the relocated people during the Three Gorges Dam project. Many southern farmers' pleas to remain on ancestral land were ignored and they were mercilessly relocated to the far north, where the climate and topography are inhospitable and completly unlike what they were used to. While "The Last Supper" works as an indictment of massive social neglect, "Report of a Work-related Injury" by Xie Xiang-nan (谢湘南, 1974–) serves as the perfect complement to "Me," a work of art by Sheng Qi (盛奇, 1963–) featured on the cover. Both point to the lack of workplace safety regulations to protect young migrant workers, many of them women from villages, who flood urban factories for low monthly wages. "Report" uses a cryptic, report-like form that is void of any emotions or empathy. "At the time of the accident/there were no witnesses." Industrialization in both poems has a double edge. It temporarily improves one's lifestyle, but the spiritual price of a vastly enhanced income is way beyond what the human mind can imagine. There is no legal team to plead on her behalf, no compensation for her mutilated hand, no assurance of further employment. The disregard for human rights at the time of China's industrialization and globalization is thoroughly captured in the cat's one simple line and the crushed fingers of the factory worker.

"The Last Supper" (最后的晚餐)

> All is ready for the last supper.
> "Be seated, please." The guest list includes
> a tiger, a goat, a cat, an elephant and
>   a Venus flytrap.

"What does each care for tonight?"
inquires the chef, a butterfly. "Nothing really
special is on the menu. Just something you've never
    tasted before."
The cat pipes up, "Too many bones in human flesh!"

最后的晚餐准备就绪
大家入座，就坐者
老虎，羚羊，老鼠，猫
大象和带嘴的植物

今晚大家最关心吃什么
厨娘蝴蝶说：没什么可招待的
就吃我们没吃过的这个吧
猫发表意见：人肉刺多

"Report of a Work-related Injury" (一起工伤事故的调查报告)

Gong Zhong-hui
Female
Twenty years old
Native of Jiangxi province
ID Number: Z0264
Department: Molding
Line of Work: Beer machine
Employment Date: 24 August 1997

While stocking beer machine,
    product fails to drop into mold
Safety door fails to open
Putting her hand in from the side
to push product down
Hand touches
safety door
Mold folds

Crushing hand
Middle finger and little finger
Two segments of middle finger, one segment of pinkie
Result of investigation:
"Violation of factory safety procedures"

Accordingly
her hands had been burned often.
Accordingly
she had been on the job for over twelve hours.
After the accident, she
accordingly
did not cry.
Neither did she
holler
holding her fingers she
staggered

At the time of the accident
there were no witnesses.

龚忠会
女
20 岁
江西吉安人
工卡号：Z0264
部门：注塑
工种：啤机
入厂时间：970824

啤塑时，产品未落，安全门
未开
从侧面伸手入模内脱
产品。手
触动

安全门
合模时
压烂
中指及无名指
中指2节，无名指一节
调查结果
属"违反工厂　　安全操作归程"

据说
她的手经常被机器烫出泡
据说
她已连续工作了十二小时
据说事发后 她
没哭　　　也没
喊叫　　她握着手指
走

事发当时无人
目睹 现场

Unlike in the early days of Communism, when writers were punished or jailed for writing satire, contemporary writers are more or less left alone. Their poems often first appeared anonymously in online chat rooms and blogs. However explicit the criticism of the party's policy, the poems were not censored nor did the authors suffer any political ramifications, a rare feat in China. How long will it be before another purification of the soul is launched?

The Poets

Yin Li-chuan
尹丽川 (1973–)

"Hidden" (掩藏)

With my mother, I always try to be fresh and youthful
I cuddle and pout, drink chicken soup, chew melon seeds
After exhausting my trick, I pretend a fever to entertain
Behind the scenes, I smoke and drink like a wretched
   old bum
Wasting away my heart and lungs

With my boyfriend, I heatedly discuss
Furniture and marriage, turn earth and heaven upside
   down fighting about the color of the bed sheets
Receive appraisal: "The lovely thing about you is
You know how to live, you have love.
Not like those crazy female poets."

On the bus I stare
at the thin backs of strangers in front of me
Suddenly tears stream down my face, I swallow the
   two dollar bills
To hide the female writer's demonic play,
I try to look radiant and dewy like jade
Smile a plump smile
   like the long-dead Mona Lisa

见母亲我永远装得鲜嫩
撒娇噘嘴，喝鸡汤磕瓜子
没辙了就感冒，哄大家开开心
转身像糟老头般酗烟酗酒
糟蹋心肺

跟男友热烈讨论
家具和婚姻，为床单的颜色吵得翻天覆地
得到评语："你可爱之处在于
懂得生活，你有爱。
不像那些疯疯颠颠的女诗人。"

在公共汽车上紧紧盯住
前排陌生人单薄的后背
突然间泪流满面，把两块钱的票根吞进胃里
为掩藏女作家那套鬼把戏，在亲人面前
我累得珠圆玉润，胖了起来
笑成了死去的蒙娜丽莎

(2003/05)

"The Old Woman" (老妇)

Every day I come downstairs to buy cigarettes
and every day I pass
by the old woman with a cart
made of bamboo, old and shabby but
good enough to hold garbage, or a child.
Is it for holding garbage, or a child?
As it is always empty
so I do not know if
she is a grandma or a scavenger.

我天天下楼买烟
老太太和她的推车
天天呆在我经过的路上
推车是竹子做的，很旧
可以装垃圾，也可以装小孩
它是用来装垃圾、还是装小孩？
它一直是空的
我不知道
她是个奶奶、还是个拾破烂的

(2000/12/4)

"Old Zhang, the Retiree" (退休工人老张)

He opened his eyes, and
for 10 minutes his eyes stared steadily at
   a nail in the ceiling.
Every dawn, for over 10 years,
   as soon as he opened his eyes
he studied that nail.
Ten years ago, the nail was in the ceiling
not in his eye.
That time as soon as he had opened his eyes,
   he would rush to work
   oh no, first to the toilet.

He has been out of work
   there is no need to rush to the toilet
so he woke up to the nail in the ceiling, and
   the nail fell into his left eye,
which cannot see the nail anymore. His right eye is still good
   but it cannot see the nail either because
there is no more nail in the ceiling.

There is a hole in the ceiling now
   like the nail in his left eye.
So his right eye is fixed on the hole in the ceiling
for a long time before the alarm o'clock
rings while the sky is still dark.

他睁开眼，天花板上
有颗钉子，他看了十分钟。
他一睁开眼，就看见天花板上，那颗钉子
有十多年了吧。
十多年前，那颗钉子，在天花板上
不在他眼里。
那时他一睁开眼，就去上班，不，先上厕所

现在他不上班，不着急去厕所，所以他醒了
就盯盯钉子。钉子掉下来，掉进了左眼
左眼坏了，看不见钉子。右眼没坏
也看不见钉子。因为天花板上，没有了钉子

天花板上，有一个洞，就像他的左眼
是一个洞。所以天花板上的洞
他是用右眼看见的。他要看上老半天
闹钟才会响，天刚蒙蒙亮了

(2000/6/18)

24

"City Thief" (城市小偷)

Grab a fistful of last year's snow[8]

squeeze it 'til it turns into a ball of clay

boundless emptiness. You can't find a rock to kick.

You have to control your hands and feet the whole way through.

The road is clean and tidy

so there is no room left for you to be bad.

The buses are no longer crowded

so you feel extremely uncomfortable.

A lady browsing for shoes says hello

and you are unaccustomed to such civility.

Neither is your stomach ready for hamburgers.

Hell! So many changes.

No one warned you ahead of time.

Big brother went to do business in Vietnam.

Second brother became a snake head.

Third brother went to the slammer.

Fourth brother died in a hit-and-run.

Fifth brother went back to the farm.

You have no place to go.

Born in 1968, you have a city residency card.

You've been self-supported since you were little.

You do not cheat or have affairs—in all, you are

More abstemious than a monk.

But whenever you pass by cops cautiously

---

8. An allusion to the fifteenth-century French poet Francois Villon (1431–63). In "Le Testament: Ballade Des Dames Du Temps Jadis," the speaker wonders, "Ou sont les neiges d'antan?" ("Where are the snows of yesteryear?"), a lamentation of the passage of time and the melancholy thought of lost beauty. It is not surprising that Yin invokes the reference of snow as she majored in French language and literature at Beijing University. Upon graduation, Yin enrolled in the French film school ESEC, and lived in France to pursue her advanced studies.

They don't even acknowledge your existence.
Your steps are slower and slower.
People swarm by you and you have to take a seat
By the city garden rail. Your ass hurts.
For the first time you doubt your profession.
All at once, you have become superfluous.
You were born, you feel, at an inopportune time.

抓一把去年的雪在手中
撮出一团黑泥后
空空如也。你找不到一颗石头踢
一路上只好手脚规矩
街面清扫得那么干净
快没有你的容身之地了
公共汽车不再拥挤
你真不习惯，卖鞋子的大姐说：
你好。你也吃不惯
包子铺里卖的汉堡
操！这么多东西变了
也没人跟你说一声
大哥去越南做大生意
二哥当了龟头，三哥进了局子
四哥被车撞死，五哥回家种地
你没处去。1968，你生于此地
你是城市户口，你从小自力更生
你不骗不盗不奸淫，你比和尚更童贞
你经过警察，小心翼翼
可人家看都不看你一眼。
你的步子越来越慢，周围人呼啦拉地
穿过你身边。你坐了下来
在城市花园，栏杆硌得你屁股生疼
第一次，你怀疑起自己深爱的职业
没有人再需要你。你生不逢时

(2000/9/30)

"Mother" (妈妈)

When I was thirteen, I asked my mother,

"What is the meaning of life?"

Following your footsteps, I entered college, too.

"Mom, what is the meaning of your life?"

Both your eyes were wide open, but

we have not spoken to each other for such a long time.

How could one woman become another's mom?

With your genes, I must continue what you did not finish doing. Mom,

you were once so beautiful, until you had me.

I began to know you little by little. You

stopped wanting to attract men's attention,

for the sake of another woman. Was it worth it, Mom?

You became a wrecked old lady, a forsaken old fan.

How could you prove that you gave birth to me, Mom?

On my way home I spotted a stooped lady with a shopping basket ahead of me.

Mom, could it be you, a mere stranger?

十三岁时我问

活着为什么你。看你上大学

我上了大学，妈妈

你活着为什么又。你的双眼还睁着

我们很久没说过话。一个女人

怎么会是另一个女人

的妈妈。带着相似的身体

我该做你没做的事么，妈妈

你曾那么地美丽，直到生下了我

自从我认识你，你不再水性杨花

为了另一个女人

你这样做得么

你成了个空虚的老太太

一把废弃的扇。什么能证明
是你生出了我，妈妈。
当我在回家的路上瞥见
一个老年妇女提着菜篮的背影
妈妈，还有谁比你更陌生

(2000/9/23)

"Orange" (橘子)

Sectioning an orange
how I wish it were you.
Just as I slice into the sphere
rendering one into two then eight pieces
You are a worm that bore into my pulp
spoiling my orange and
my mouth-watering
sweet and sour life.

手刃一个橘子
我多想手刃你
多想你就是一个橘子
就像我手刃这个橘子
一瓣两瓣八瓣
你是橘子里的虫子
你毁了我的橘子
毁了我酸甜可口的生活

(2000/10/22)

"Lover" (情人)

Now, you come
fondle me, hug me, chew my breasts
bite me, and smack my face
all are futile now.
Whatever you do
they are but copycats. The old we
fill the room with heat, and you with your sweat.
We were both strong, pushing harder and harder.
Nothing could separate us except old age.
But who would imagine
it coming on so fast?

这时候，你过来
摸我、抱我、咬我的乳房
吃我、打我的耳光
都没用了
这时候，我们再怎样
都是在模仿，从前的我们
屋里很热，你都出汗了
我们很用劲儿。比从前更用劲儿。
除了老，谁也不能
把我们分开。这么快
我们就成了这个样子

(2000/7/31)

"Passing by the Workers" (经过民工)

Squatting, cradling big bowls, they devour their lunch
flanking both sides of the street and I
   part them up the middle
My cell phone rings and I quicken my steps
my limbs inside my taut mini skirt
   feel relaxed
my bare breasts beneath my shirt too
my tense, self-conscious expression betrays me
   though no one notices me.
They fix their gazes only
   upon the cabbage, potato, and two pieces of
   meat in their bowl.

他们正在吃饭，蹲着，端着大碗
马路一边一排，我就要从中间经过了
手机响了，我步伐从容
我裹在超短裙里的下半身从容
我没有穿内衣的上半身也从容
表情专注得过分。明明没有人看我
大白菜、土豆、两块肥肉

(2000/8/3)

"Hand" (手)

Year long your hand is buried in the cabbage basket
   searching for the roundest one,
   but they all cost the same
   just one dollar.
Your hand is stained, forever, and greasy from
Mopping the dining room table.
Picking up your needle work, you catch your daughter's
   reprimand
"Turn off that TV, will ya, Ma! I am doing my homework."
You busy your hands with—nothing now.
Those hands had clutched at your husband's shirt tail.
He never did leave but eternally disdains you.
Your children are grown and your hands cradle your
   grandchildren
Until the hired nanny arrived to replace you.
"Ma, all your life you toiled yourself. Try enjoying life a little."
Your hands reach out to your son, and catch nothing.
He leaves for work and you perch on the window sill
   looking down from the high rise over a sea of flagging
   laundry on lines
your ten fingers stretched out in front of you,
you see the years slipping through them
you don't know
this afternoon until twilight descended
what to do.

你的手常年在一筐圆白菜中
找出最值的那个。都是一块钱，
你可有三个孩子。你的手在食堂
擦几十张饭桌。油腻是洗不掉的了
回家拿起毛衣针，女儿还皱眉：
妈，把电视关了，我在做功课。
你的手忙来忙去，扯住丈夫的衣角
丈夫最终没走，比以前更瞧你不起。
儿女们大了，你手里捧着孙子
直到来了，身强体壮的保姆。妈，
您就别操心了，儿子说，累了一辈子，该
享福。你伸手想摸摸儿子的脸
扑空了。儿子出门办公了。
你讪讪地笑着，坐到窗边
俯视这个城市飘扬的尿布。你张开十指
你都忘了，这些年怎么能就这样
从指缝中流走。你不知道
今天下午，应该做些什么，直到天黑

(2000/8/2)

"Chinese Rap" (中式RAP)

Love is not love when you mix it with hate
Revolution is not real when you demand to know the cause
La la la la la la la
xi li and hua la

What is love and what is revolution?
Love is a never-ending revolution
Revolution is a love-to-the-death affair!
Love ya love ya love ya love
fame ya rev ya rev ya fame!
Love is wet, rev is dry and
soon as you're wet, you revolt and dry
once you dry you start to revolt
rev ya rev ya brother sit!
sit ya sit ya do it brother!
sit till your wineglass cracks
   make love till love is dry![9]

有了缘故的爱恨不是我的爱情
有了缘故的革命不是真的革命。
啦啦啦啦啦啦啦
稀里又哗啦

什么是爱情？什么是革命？
爱情是一条革不完的命
革命是一次爱到死的情！
爱呀爱呀爱呀爱
名呀命呀命呀名！
爱情是湿的，革命是干的

---

9. A pun is formed by the words for "sit" (坐) and "make" (做) which are both pronounced *zuo* with the same falling tone. The Chinese word for "hole," translated as the wineglass "crack," is pronounced *chuan* and that for "dry" is *gan* so these two rhyme in Chinese.

一湿你就干，一干它就干。

革呀革呀哥呀坐

坐呀坐呀做呀哥

把酒杯坐穿！把爱情做干！

(2000/02/18)

"Vase" (花瓶)

Must be some horses

wanting to go back to the ancient past

like some people nostalgic for silent films

like some fresh flowers

longing so much to wither and shrivel

that they want to be put in a vase

like that vase

   pale, round, so serene

   evenly covered with dust

    how tender and poignant, that film of ash.

一定有一些马

想回到古代

就像一些人怀恋默片

就像一些鲜花

渴望干燥和枯萎

好插进花瓶

就像那个花瓶白白的园园的那么安静

(2003/05/13)

"Remembering New Zealand" (想起新西兰)

The killer's hand
is white like the lotus
white like the white of the lotus
"Having killed, the hand cannot be changed"
That belongs to Gu Cheng[10]
Gu Cheng belongs to the poets
He isn't man's
Excuses are for the dead
The hand of the killer is a lotus
when in a tight fist
an axe when open
The palm of the axe runs red
The wrinkles of the palm vanish.

杀人的人的手
像荷花一样白
荷花洁白的白
"杀了，手是不能换的"
这是顾城的
顾城是诗人的
他不是男人的
借口是死人的
凶手的行凶的手
攥紧是荷花
张开是斧头
斧心潮红
掌纹不见

(2003/05/09)

---

10. Gu Cheng was a highly acclaimed member of China's Second Generation poets.

"Cause and Effect" (因果)

For popcorn,
the corn can't refuse to grow.
For summer,
the melon man lifts his knife.

When the scholar puts down his knife,
he becomes a genius.
When peasants put down their knives,
they're still peasants.
When gangsters put down their knives,
they're politicians.[11]
When the monk raises his,
he's striving for fame.

For the children to die of hunger
and the girls to die of old age,
that year Hebei[12] had a drought.

To erase evidence of the corpse
they spread the mildew
and it rained for ten years in the capital city.

---

11. This line is a parody of a well-known Chinese idiom: 放下屠刀，立地成佛" when one puts down the knife, one becomes a Buddha," meaning that a wrongdoer achives salvation as soon as he gives up evil. But the poet substitutes "politician" for Buddha to emphasize the notorious reputation of Chinese politicians, who pretend to be well meaning but underneath are still evil.

12. Hebei is a province bordering southern Beijing

为了爆米花
玉米不得不生长
为了夏天
卖瓜的汉子
举起了刀

书生放下了刀
成为精英
农民放下了刀
还是农民
黑手党放下了刀
他们是政客
佛举起了刀
他想出名

为了饿死孩子
老死姑娘
这一年
河北大旱
为了毁尸灭迹
滋养梅毒
京城十年
一直下雨

(2002/04/25)

Tan Ke-xiu
谭克修 (1971–)

"Empty" (空空荡荡)

Their room so empty. Those
unnamable columns, squares, wood planks
still clinging tight together
completing the lonely vacant silence
   of their twilight years.
The main room can't hold a gust of wind,
which has come a long way, from entering
   my bedroom looking for last year's scar
on my plaid bedspread. The walls are bare.
Only an old clock, still pacing on tiptoe
in the corners of time
watching the wood's color secretly darken.

Their clothes so empty. The inches fallen
on the years, surrendering to the cool breezes drifting.
I see the pear tree behind the house. Its fruits
fallen, the birds flown, leaving
dry branches shaking in the moonlit cold,
empty beneath its slacken bark.
He's given even his bad temper to his children.
She's given her most secret longings to the gods.
Only a little arthritis and a bit of cough live
in their endlessly bent bodies.

Their nights so empty. Only a scattering
of stars and baying of dogs, a light
in the far darkness attends decreasing sleep.
Their sleep so empty, their thinning dreams
like a thin cloud floating by
the long dried fields.
Their dreams so empty, just a bunch of old,
used-up days swaying inside the body like the dark cars
   of a train,
toward a mysterious slice of territory.
Toward the empty me.

他们的房子空空荡荡。这些
叫不出名字的木柱，木方，木板
依然紧紧地抱在一起
围合着他们晚年的空虚和寂静
偌大的堂屋坐不稳一束远道而来的
风，在我卧房的方格床单上找寻着
去年的折痕。墙壁上空空荡荡
只有一座老式挂钟，依然
踮着脚尖在时间的角落里徘徊
眼看着木头的颜色在暗暗加深

他们的衣服空空荡荡。向年龄
陷下去的尺寸，让位给了阵阵的
凉风。我看见屋后的梨树，果实
已经落下，叶子和鸟儿已经飞走
留下干枯的枝桠晃动着腊月的寒冷
他们松驰的皮肤里空空荡荡
连他暴躁的脾气也交给了子女
连她隐秘的愿望也交给了神灵
他们不断下弯的身子
只住着小小的风湿和咳嗽

他们的夜晚空空荡荡。只有零散的
星子和犬吠，在遥远的黑暗中
闪烁，搅拌着愈来愈少的睡眠
睡眠空空荡荡，愈来愈稀薄的梦
就像久旱的田野中偶尔飘过
一片稀薄的云影。梦里空空荡荡
都是一些用旧了的日子，仿佛
一结结幽暗的车厢，在体内
晃晃悠悠地行使，朝着某片
神秘的领域。朝着空空荡荡的我

Yu Xiang
宇向 (1970–)

"The Sun Shines Where It Needs To" (阳光照在需要它的地方)

The sun shines where it needs to
shines on the sunflowers and the street
shines on more sunflower-like flora
shines on more street-like places.
Between happy or unhappy couples,
on the street where it rained last night
it's as if the sun shone directly through
shining on the panties and bras on the balcony
and the renovated sign on the bathroom door
shining on the cold and the dripping beads of sweat
shining in the August sky, the almost glassless glass
the almost not-crying child
shining on the crying child
    but it won't shine into his childhood.
Shining in my eyes but it won't shine through my hands,
it won't shine on the back of the door
    it won't shine on the adulterous lovers.
The sun is not where it's not needed.

The sun never shines where it is not needed
The sun shines on my body,
sometimes, it doesn't
    shine on me.

阳光照在需要它的地方
照在向日葵和马路上
照在更多向日葵一样的植物上
照在更多马路一样的地方
在幸福与不幸的夫妻之间
在昨夜下过大雨的街上
阳光几乎垂直照过去
照着阳台上的内裤和胸衣
洗脚房装饰一新的门牌
照着寒冷也照着滚落的汗珠
照着八月的天空，几乎没有玻璃的玻璃
几乎没有哭泣的孩子
照到哭泣的孩子却照不到一个人的童年
照到我眼上照不到我的手
照不到门的后面照不到偷情的恋人
阳光不在不需要它的地方

阳光从来不照在不需要它的地方
阳光照在我身上
有时它不照在我身上

"Just Thinking That" (我真的这样想)

I want to hug you.
Right now, my right hand's draped on my left shoulder
my left hand's draped on my right shoulder.
I only want to hug you. My chin sinks into my chest
just thinking so.
Now, you're standing in front of me.
I want so much
to hug you, hug you
   desperately and hard.
My two hands start holding my shoulders even harder
just thinking so.

我想拥抱你
现在，我的右手搭在我的左肩
我的左手搭在我的右肩上
我只想拥抱你，我想着
下巴就垂到胸口
现在，你就站在我的面前
我多想拥抱你
迫切地紧紧地拥抱你
我这样想
我的双手就更紧地抱住了我的双肩

"2002, I Have" (2002, 我有)

I have a door on which it's written:
Warning: You may become lost!
I have several pieces of paper, the kind without lines
that records my shameless verse
and I don't know where the good times have gone.
Instead I'm left with a shriveled wallet and a bit of talent
If I were an obedient girl
I would be a good daughter, good citizen, good lover
I would
   chuck my freedom out the window and never write
   another poem.
But I'm a disgusting person
with dirty feet and discount scarf
that make my man a real man
make him happy, brave, suddenly in love with life
I have a real man. I have
arms I use to embrace. I have
a right hand I use to squeeze, to throw things,
   to shake hands with strangers.
I have a left hand I use to caress and love,
yet where did those painful affairs go?
Those entanglements, extra key rings.
I have cigarettes to blacken my lungs, yellow
my fingers. I have the light of self-knowledge.
   I have passion and I have wounds. I have
electricity. You'd be happy if it sets you on fire.
I have a place to hide and a P.O. box. I have
birth control pills and sleeping pills. I have
a phone, red like lust. I have
a habit of dialing numbers. I have heard
enough of its rings. Why do I always call
places where no one picks up?

我有一扇门上面写着：
当心！ 你也许会迷路
我有几张纸，不带格子的那种
记满我没有羞涩的句子
而我有过的好时光不知哪里去了
我有一个瘪瘪的钱包和一点点才能
如果我做一个乖乖女
就会是一个好女儿，好公民，好恋人
我就丢了自由并不会写诗
而我是一个污秽的人，有一双脏脚和一条廉价围巾
这使我的男人成为真正的男人
使他幸福，勇敢，突然就爱上了生活
我有一个真正的男人
我有手臂，用来拥抱
我有右手，用来握用来扔用来接触生人
我有左手，我用它抚摸和爱
而那些痛苦的事情都哪里去了
那些纠葛，多余的钥匙环和公式
我有香烟染黑肺，染黄手指
我有自知之明，我有狂热也有伤口
我有电，如果你被击痛你就快乐了
我有藏身之处，有长密码的邮箱
我有避孕药和安眠药
我有一部 电话，它红得像欲望
我有拨号码的习惯，我听够了震铃声
为什么我总是把号码拨到
一个没人接电话的地方

Liu Chun
刘春 (1970–)

"Purity" (纯洁)

When it emerged on paper as an expression,
   even if only once
it will become its own enemy.
Nothing as white as a piece of paper, then there's nothing
like a first poem carved into his heart and bones.

That was his wish, but it's long since vanished
like the short romances of youth.
The same piece of paper, yet in another's hand it's imprinted
   with grandeur
The same type of human, yet your counterpart holds
   a government seal.

One person leaves himself, becomes another.
His past clean, but ashamed to speak.
His present mediocre, but eager to add vacuous pretenses.
—In times of pain, he expertly hides his wound.

Yes, before he understood silence, he learned to hide,
Rubbing his glasses with a piece of paper, not to polish them
but to make them thinner, to distort their precision.
His life, too, would be rubbed into nothing.

Maybe after a number of years, he would choose
an evening, face the setting sun and mumble to himself
sunning out those words he should long have spoken.

    The past
buried too deep, repressed too long,
    as if they were natural.

Now middle-aged expecting a son
at month's end, he studies a father's homework
but uneasy, knowing nothing more
than a newborn.

当它以表意的方式呈现在纸上，即使只有一次
它也将成为自己的敌人。没有什么
比一张纸更白。正如
没有什么比第一首诗更让他刻骨铭心

那曾经是他的梦想，但已过早地消逝
一如青春期短暂的爱情
同样是纸，但别人手上的印着伟人头像
同样是人，但对方持有一枚公章

一个人离开了自己，成为另一个
他的过去是清白的，但羞于说出口
他的现在是庸碌的，但需要加入一些虚伪
    疼痛时，恰到好处地捂住伤口

是的，懂得沉默之前，他学会了掩饰
用纸摩擦眼镜片上的水气，不是为了更明亮
而是让它变薄，失去准确度
他也会在与生活的摩擦中耗尽一生

或许若干年后，他会选择一个黄昏
面对夕阳喃喃自语，晾晒一些
早该说出的话语，那些往事
埋藏得太深，压抑得太久，如同人性本身

而现在他还是中年，他的孩子
将在一个月后降临，他在学习一个父亲的功课
但心情忐忑，　　对于生活
先知也不比一个婴儿知道得更多

"An Earthly Morning" (一个俗人的早晨)

Passing the dense forest one morning,
I heard the trees conversing, their breathing
gentle and modest. If it were winter, I'd imagine
that their whispers were white feathers falling.
But it was May, the air warm, and people in the city
in light clothing.
And so I, filled with idle thoughts, imagining
them as a group warming
one another with a little imagination, a little lie.
In the mist their outlines emerged.
Finally I saw their shape: slender, independent,
ethereal.

A mortal had no right
   to speak in such an innocent morning,
like the children spotting the fox goddess
in the mountain and unable to make a sound.
Sometimes I, too, imitate the trees and stand in silence,
to become myself.
But nature would soon discover my flaws ——
just a little time, and my waist would
bend without any will.
Just a little hunger, and my appetite would
stretch out countless desperate fingers.

从树林边走过，在清晨
我听到树木在交谈，它们的呼吸
轻柔恬淡，如果是冬天
我会幻想那是它们身上飘落的白色羽毛
而这是五月，天气状况
已允许市民穿着单衣
我因此有了闲情。
我原以为它们是一个群体
靠一些理想，一些谎言相互取暖
雾气中，轮廓逐渐清晰
最后，我看到它们的样子：清瘦，独立
仙风道骨

一个俗人无权在这个纯洁的早晨说话
像山里的孩子看到狐仙
发不出一丝声响。
有时候，我也会学着树木的样子
静静站立，想成为自己
而大地看出了的破绽
只需一点时间
我的腰身就会不由自主地弯曲
只需一点饥饿
我的体内就会伸出无数只手指

Zhu Qing-he
朱庆和 (1973–)

"After the Rain" (雨后的事情)

First there were four,
later a few more
They stood in a line on the street
the rain had just washed clean
They were smoking, talking
   about things like playing cards
The cigarette smoke was light, so it faded quickly
The rice field was green
The distant jungle so green it was almost black
They started to talk about girls, wishing
a pretty one would come to them from afar
clothes dripping wet
and everyone would say something to her
They were thinking about what they should say
and just as they had hoped
they saw a pretty girl walking
   toward them from afar

先是四个人，后来
又多了几个
他们一律站在路边上
路面被雨水冲刷得干净
他们抽着烟，说着打牌的事
烟很轻，随即就散掉了
稻田是绿色的
远处的树林也绿得发黑

他们谈起了姑娘
他们希望有一个漂亮的姑娘从远处走过来
而且身上湿淋淋的
大家都想对她说点什么
他们在想该对她说点什么好呢
正如他们所希望的，就看见
姑娘真的从远处走了过来

"The Grape Seller" (卖葡萄的男人)

The grape seller balances his baskets on a yoke
    walking across the street
The ear cleaner calls him over to the sidewalk
The grape seller hears her, but only after awhile.
"The grapes are fresh. Buy more if you want them."

"Your ears are no good. You'd better first come and
    unclog them."
The grape seller puts down his baskets
It's as the ear cleaner said: his ears can't hear
Looking at her hands, you know she's good at her craft.
"Look. Look. So much ear wax!
Take it home and use it to fertilize your grapes.
    They'll grow even fatter."
A boy steals some grapes
The grape seller wants to chase after him.

The ear cleaner says, "Don't move, otherwise
your eardrum will break and you really won't hear."
The grape seller had no choice but to stay still, not move
    a muscle.
"That child's truly hungry. Let him eat."

The woman says, "OK, now you can hear whatever you
    want to hear."
The grape seller stands up and gives a listen. Then gives her
    two bunches of grapes.

卖葡萄的男人挑着担子在街上走着
掏耳朵的女人站在街边喊他过去
连喊了几声，卖葡萄的男人才听见
葡萄是刚摘的，要买就多买些吧

你耳朵不好使，还是先来掏掏耳朵
卖葡萄的男人放下了担子
掏耳朵的女人说得真不错
耳朵是听不清了，看那双手就知道技术不错
你瞧，你瞧，耳屎这么多
回家给你的葡萄当肥料，会长得更大些
一个男孩偷走了葡萄，就站在不远的地方
卖葡萄的男人想站起来追

掏耳朵的女人说，千万别动
不然耳膜会破，那样可就真听不见了
卖葡萄的男人只好一动不动
那个孩子或许是真哦了，就让他吃吧

女人说一声好了，你现在想听什么就听什么
男人起身听了听，然后送了她两串葡萄

Hu Xu-Dong
胡续东 (1974–)

"Snowy Night" (雪夜)

Many years ago, whenever it snowed at night, I would
down a mouthful of whiskey, change the rooster
  in my throat
into a wrathful bull. Let him wind up and bellow,
"Let me let off some steam in the snow!"
His head charged into the school's enchanted silence
against the snowstorm, blind to the matador
leaving patches of disturbance in the snow.
It's a snowy night again where the school's silence
still seems enchanted, intangible.
I'm nearly thirty. I neither drink nor bellow.
In a body full of old illnesses, I turn right, another right,
trailing the silence to the last right.

"A bout of good snow can bring out a lifetime's
normal insecurity and dishonesty."
Remembering an unfinished poem
  with a doomed beginning, I lifted my head
and saw the fat snowflakes leisurely falling, reflecting
the golden street lamp light, its rich aura
  gaudily carpeting the dirty street.
But I know,
  In the quietest left corner of this enchanted palace,
  from the thinnest, weakest snowflake,
will rush out a handsome bull, rushing away the cold
  on my lung,
grieving over the dead matador trampled there.

多年前，一到下雪的夜晚，我就会
灌几口大嗓门的烈酒，把桑子里的公鸭
灌成一头愤怒的公牛，让它铆足了劲，
吼着"快让我在雪地上撒点野"，一头
扎进校园里迷宫一样的安静之中，去抵撞
扑面而来的雪片里看不见的斗牛士，在雪地上
留下大片大片的蛮力。而今，又逢雪夜，
校园里的安静依旧如迷宫一般
不可促摸，我年近三十，不喝酒，也不想吼，
裹着一身宿疾，向右转，再向右转，走在安静
的最后边。

"一场好雪能够下出一个人一生所必需的
恰当的自卑和不诚实。"我想起数天前
一首未竟之作失败的开头，抬头看见
路灯下肥大的雪片在安闲地飘洒，闪着金光，
喘着财气，大摇大摆地落在肮脏的地面。
但我知道，在迷宫最安静的左边，一定会从
一片瘦弱的雪花里冲出一头精壮的公牛，它将闯进
我肺叶上的冷，去哀悼死在那里的斗牛士。

Jiang Fei
江非 (1974–)

"The Roofer" (干零工的泥瓦匠)

"To reach the roof, I'll need a ladder.
How else would I get up there
to change the cracked tile?"

Father goes to find a ladder.

"Not only do I need a ladder. I'll need
a new piece of tile, of course. The broken one
needs to be taken down and changed immediately
for a new one."

Father goes into town to find a tile.

"The tile is here.
but I'm missing the putty."

Father reaches up to the roof and brings one down.

"Now I'm missing a rope."

Father takes down the quilted jacket from the clothesline.

"One last thing missing is a little mud."

Father casually digs a few shovels' full in the yard
piles up a small amount of dirt
throws a bit of water on it.

He says, "Good. Just like that."
And like a monkey climbs up on our roof.

But to our surprise, when he reaches the top,
the guy actually asks, "Where's the problem?"

This time, father can't think of any way to help him,
so he cheerfully moves the ladder away.

爬上屋顶要有梯子
不然，我怎么上去
换下那块毁坏的瓦砾

父亲去找梯子。

有了梯子还不行
还要有一块新瓦
当然，碎的拿下来了
要赶紧换上新的

父亲又匆匆到镇上去买脊瓦

脊瓦买回来
还缺一把抹子

父亲伸手从屋檐上抽了下来。

又缺一根绳子

父亲取下晾衣绳子上的棉衣。

最后缺的是泥巴

父亲就在院子里随便铲了几下

堆起一个小土堆
洒了点水。

他说，好了
就这样，然后像一只猴子那样
蹿上了我们的房顶

可是，没料想，到了上面
这家伙竟然又问，问题出在哪里

这一次，父亲已想不出怎样才能帮上他
于是乐呵呵地移走了屋檐上的梯子。

"The Woodsman" (劈柴的那个人还在劈柴)

Hack, crack, thwack
the woodsman chopped deep into the evening.
The firewood piled up
like a mountain in front of him.

Thwack, the woodsman continued

one hand resting on the ax handle
the other steadying the log
Down came the ax in a swift arc
squeaking, cracking fell asunder the quartered cedar and elm

Like this
the woodsman pounded on well into the dark

I don't recall which winter it was
I was a spectator then
observing every movement
I uttered softly, occasionally
    "Dad"

He heard me
and lifted his head, smiling
    toward me
then went back to splitting the cord

The following day
a heavy snowfall covered
the mound of firewood.

劈柴的那个人还在劈柴
他已经整整劈了一个下午
那些劈碎的柴木
已在他面前堆起了一座小山

可是他还在劈

他一手拄着斧头
另一只手把一截木桩放好
然后
抡起斧子向下砸去
木桩发出咔嚓撕裂的声音

就这样
那个劈柴的人一直劈到了天黑

我已忘记了这是哪一年冬天的情景
那时我是一个旁观者
我站在边上看着那个人劈柴的姿势
有时会小声地喊他一声父亲
他听见了
会抬起头冲我笑笑
然后继续劈柴

第二天
所有的新柴
都将被大雪覆盖

"The Prickly Pepper Tree" (花椒木)

Once at dusk I chopped firewood
on New Year's Day
or was it New Year's eve?
the weather was turning colder and
a stranger was arriving at the inn
so I needed to split enough before dawn

I did not exert much effort
just slightly lifting the ax
not like my father
clenching his teeth, aiming a full swing
at each log's core,
heaving

I gathered quarters
of elm, willow, and poplar
well seasoned timber
the remains of the day
bundled randomly

I lightly lodged my ax
  into the weathered segment
as if entering time's crevices
forcing the edge deeper
into time's annulated precipice

My mind went to the guest at the inn
stopping by a prickly pepper tree
old and forgotten
once scarred by father's blade and
mercifully left behind for today

The prickly pepper retained its shape
as if
time's hatchet feared its thorny armor
and hesitated to enter the prickly pepper tree

as though time had halted
in the face of resistance
I split and stacked well into the dark
ripping time into smithereens
the guest had reached his destination
a loving stranger stopping mid-journey
for warmth and affection.

有一年，我在黄昏里劈柴
那是新年，或者
新年的前一天
天更冷了，有一个陌生人
要来造访
我提前要在我的黄昏里劈取一些新的柴木

劈柴的时候
我没有过多的用力
只是低低地举起镐头
也没有像父亲那样
咬紧牙关
全身地扑下去，呼气

我只是先找来了一些木头
榆木、槐木和杨木
它们都是废弃多年的木料
把这些剩余的时光
混杂地拢在一起

我轻轻地把镐头伸进去
像伸进一条时光的缝隙
再深入一些
碰到了时光的峭壁

我想着那个还在路上的陌生人
在一块花椒木上停了下来
那是一块很老的木头了
当年父亲曾经劈过它
但是不知为什么却留了下来

它的样子，还是从前的
没有发生任何改变
好像时光也惧怕花椒的气息
没有做任何的深入

好像时光也要停了下来
面对一个呛鼻的敌人
我在黄昏里劈着那些柴木
那些时光的碎片
好像那个陌生人，已经来了
但是一个深情的人，在取暖的路上
深情地停了下来

Yang Chun-min
杨春民 (1979–)

"Distant Relatives" (远房亲戚)

> *Far from a cultural centre he was used:*
> *Abandoned by his general and his lice,*
> *Under a padded quilt he turned to ice*
> *And vanished. He will never be perused.*

He didn't know the good, didn't follow the good, but he taught it to us.[13]

——W. H. Auden (Sonnets from China, Number 13)

One day when I was young, a bunch of relatives from far away came to visit. Father treated them warmly, sat cross-legged chatting and smoking with them in the house like old friends. Among them was a strange person who started to attract my attention. One of his hands had only four fingers!

I was filled with curiosity about that injured hand, but too afraid of the idea of pain and brutality, I could only sneak glimpses of him and his fingers from a distance. This distant relative finally noticed me, smiled, raised his hand to say hello. I was so scared that I ran to my mother's side, trembling from head to toe.

Everyone laughed. Mother told me that he was a distant uncle who, to avoid fighting the enemy, cut off his right thumb.

---

13. This line is not Auden's, but added by the poet.

Time has a way of blurring the neglected and the trespasses
in our memory. I can't remember now that group of distant
relatives, the complicated relations and their places in my
bloodline.
That's the mistake we make toward our fathers' generation
and history.

Every time I question history and our lives, a hand with a miss-
ing finger rises to warn me:
Only because of an unwillingness to die for nothing. What
kind of determination and courage allowed him to bear that
sharp pain and a lifetime of difficulty?

What kind of cowardice and lies led him to transcend
words and honor and
history's convoluted truth until he himself couldn't trust
  good and justice and the simple truth
of his own body?

他被使用在远离文化中心的地方，
又被他的将军和他的虱子所遗弃，
于是在一件棉袄里他闭上眼睛
而离开人世。人家不会把他提起。
。 。 。 。 。 。
他不知善，不择善，却教育了我们
　　W. H. Auden (战时十四行诗，第十三首)

小时候的一天，一群亲戚从远方
来到了家里做客。父亲对他们很是亲热
在屋里和他们一起盘腿坐着
抽着烟，像老朋友一样聊着天。
在他们当中，一位奇怪的人
开始引起了我的注意：
他的一只手上，只有四个手指！

我对那只残缺的手掌充满着好奇
但对疼痛和残忍的想象与恐惧
使我只敢在远处偷偷地
凝视着他和他的手指
那远房亲戚最后也发现了我
便笑着用手和我打了打招呼
我感到非常害怕
迅速转身跑到了母亲的身旁
大人们这时一起轰声大笑。
母亲告诉我，他是我的一位远房表叔
为了不被抓作壮丁去和敌人作战
他砍掉了右手的一根拇指。
时间对一切的遗忘和超越
模糊的记忆里
我现在已经记不清那群远房亲戚
与我在血缘上的排列
以及那些烦琐的亲疏
这是我们对父辈和历史常常犯下的疏忽

每当我对历史与人生产生疑惑
一只残缺的手掌总警示着我：
只是不愿了去白白送死
一种什么样的决心和勇气
能使他忍受卑劣的痛苦和一生的不便
一个什么样的怯懦和欺骗
确使他超越了言辞的道德
和历史复杂的真相
成为 了他自己没有意识到的
善和正义，以及真理简单的自身

Shi Yi-long
石一龙 (1976–)

"Empty Fortress" (空城)

I suspect that his vision on the road
of the world has been frozen. Who has
built the fortress ahead? Someone answers.
He and I will always be at odds.

I can't denounce anyone who's been
  to the fortress.
As if he'd lost his senses,
dazed and aggrieved, he climbed to the very top,
and facing the cold wall, he forgot the world's
dark, dark crowds, the painted puppets.
And those wearing masks with hair adrift—
  they were partying.
I suspect Kafka's writing. I suspect
he plagiarized the verses on the fortress wall.
By the main castle gate stands a singing poet.
In the honest shadow of the sun
plays the innocent child
Its strong and loud clatter despises me.
The grand fortress has a pair of eyes
stand solitary from the darkness of the world.
I shout, "I'll definitely conquer you!"
Before me stands the empty fortress
whose sounds of laughter follow me.

他的目光在大世界的路上
我怀疑被冰冻了
前面是谁筑起的城堡　一个人回答出
我和他永远隔膜

我无法斥责走进城堡的任何人
仿佛失去知觉　　　　呆滞而且悲痛
走上顶端
他忘了世界上黑压压的群
面对冷漠的墙壁，伪装的纸人和戴面具的
人瑟瑟发抖的头发　　他们狂欢
我怀疑卡夫卡的写作
他是否抄袭了城堡里的词语
大门的入口站着一个颂诗者
阳光朴实的背面
嬉戏奔跑的儿童　　　铿然有声
它的声音轻视了我
华丽的城堡有一双眼睛
它与世界的黑夜隔阂
我大喊，我一定征服你
我的前面是一座空城
他的嘲笑紧紧相随

Ma Fei
马非 (1971–)

"The Last Supper" (最后的晚餐)

All is ready for the last supper.
"Be seated, please." The guest list includes
a tiger, a goat, a cat, an elephant and
a Venus flytrap.

"What does each care for tonight?"
inquires the chef, a butterfly. "Nothing really
special is on the menu. Just something you've never
    tasted before."
The cat pipes up, "Too many bones in human flesh!"

最后的晚餐准备就绪
大家入座，就坐者
老虎，羚羊，老鼠，猫
大象和带嘴的植物

今晚大家最关心吃什么
厨娘蝴蝶说：没什么可招待的
就吃我们没吃过的这个吧
猫发表意见：人肉刺多

Huang Jin-ming
黄金明 (1974–)

"Old Hutong[14] Lament" (街的伤感之歌)

The rain continues to pour. The dispirited street
turns muddy. Rain drops come down
like needles, pricking my leather sole.
The noon-time darkness blows,
like a pandemic
into the autumn lung.
Let me take away this tired *hutong*, to the prairie,
to the wilderness, to the damp
rented room.
The pub scatters the scent of love, barbecued lamb
and some Er-guo-tou.[15] Let me
raise a toast to the little town,
to the street bums, to the soldier-like trees standing sentry.
Get them all drunk!
Let me become the needle on an old gramophone
time and again scratching the scarred sound track
my adolescent love sharp as fish hooks.
Let me
become a wild clock
with broken springs, sinking into time's oblivion.
The rain continues to fall.

---

14. A *hutong* is a narrow alleyway or street.

15. *Er-guo-tou* is a Chinese rice liquor as strong as, if not stronger than, vodka.

Like a crow, I let the rain
wash off shameful memories, shake off
my eye sockets' dark circles. Let me
present a drunken rose to
my poor village and to
her mothers and fathers.
An old alley with its base and trivial charm, its stale scent
a romantic song drifts from a wooden radio frame
a lover's quarrel carries over from next door
an old alley, how much crowded childhood you hold!
A group of youngsters splashes in the street gutters,
and blurs my vision. Let me
be a bald old man who plays his old wife
a sad tune
The rain continues to fall.
Let me be a trash bin,
kicked over by a drunkard, spilling my poem:
this repressive thunder, this rotten lightning!

雨一直在下，颓废的街道
开始变得泥泞。雨点像钉子
撒落了一地，我的皮鞋
被刺穿了。正午的黑暗
像一场疾病吹入了
秋天的肺部。让我把这条疲倦的
小街带走，带到郊外
阒寂的旷野，带到潮湿的
出租屋。小酒馆散发出
情欲的滋味，烤羊肉正好
适合下二锅头。请让我
把这座城市灌醉，把街头的
流浪汉灌醉，把哨兵一样的
街道树痛痛灌醉！请让我

成为一张旧唱片的指针
一次次划过音乐的伤口
我年少时的爱情，锐利如
喉咙间的鱼钩。请让我
成为一只狂妄的闹钟
把发条卸掉，追入时间的
深渊。雨一直在下
我像一只乌鸦，在雨中
洗掉屈辱的记忆，抖落
眼眶的铁锈。请让我
把一株喝醉的玫瑰
护送回贫穷的乡村
交给她的父母。一条老街
有它庸俗和琐屑的美，有它
永不飘散的气味。木壳收音机
荡漾着邓丽君的歌声，隔壁传来
一对年轻夫妇的争吵。一条老街
埋葬了多少密集的童年！一群孩子
在雨水中奔跑，我来不及
看清他们的身影。请让我
像那位秃顶的老头，对着老伴
拉响呜咽的胡琴。雨一直在下
请让我像路边的垃圾桶
被醉鬼一脚踢翻，倾倒出心底的诗篇：
这暗哑的雷霆，这腐烂的闪电！

Sheng Xing
盛兴 (1978–)

"Sleeping Pills" (安眠药)

> Those friends of mine
> mix their pills like stirring coffee
> sip after sip
> then bottoms up.
> Shrugging their shoulders,
> their posture
> like a suit of armor,
> they are invincible tonight.
>
> We bump into each other sometimes on our way
> to the pharmacy. Nodding knowingly we enter
> our separate
>   sleepless nights.
>
> "You cannot buy the pills in bulk.
> You will arouse suspicion!"
>
> But the sum of the pills consumed,
> our grand total, is enough to
>   kill the entire light in the dark
> save the entire darkness in a white night.
>
> In those days,
> dragging our mismatched shoes to and fro
> sometimes we toast
> our days and nights
> shooting the breeze

feeling the transition between sober and drowsy moments
searching the horizon between time
lost and other days.

我的那些朋友们
将安眠药咖啡般轻轻搅匀
一口一口地小啜
剩在杯底的部分一饮而尽
象我摊一摊手
他们端着杯子的姿势
像一只坚硬的盾牌
在夜晚无懈可击

有时我们在去药店的路上相遇
彼此摇一摇头
就进入各自没有安眠药无法入睡的黑夜

你不能同时买下大量的药
你将遭到猜忌与拒绝无疑

而这些年我们所食安眠药的总和
足可以杀死一整个黑夜里的光明
救活一整个白昼里的黑夜也足够

在那些光阴里
我们托着无法成双的鞋子
在卧室趿来趿去
有时也举杯祝愿
彼此的黑夜与白天
杯子干了以后就聊一些与睡眠无关的话题
感受着睡意与清醒间的过渡
寻找着虚度了的岁月
与其他岁月的界线

Song Lie-yi
宋烈毅 (1973–)

"Rope Tale" (绳子的故事)

>One rope, two suicides
>two attempts, only one
>rope can't be used twice.
>
>Two ropes, one person in despair
>Before, it was just one rope, now cut into
>two
>two ropes can't be given to just one person who wants to
>kill himself.
>
>Give two ropes to two people
>but don't give them
>two
>chances at one time.
>
>The dilemma of two ropes available one at a time
>one person wanting to do it twice with one rope
>another wanting to do it once with two ropes
>
>The rope snaps.

一根绳子　　两个自杀的人

两次企图　　遇上了一根

不能重复使用两次的绳子

两根绳子　　曾经是一个

绝望的人　　曾经是一根绳子

一根绳子　　分成了两根绳子

两根绳子　　不能给一个人

想要自杀的人　　　　给两个人

两根绳子　　也不能同时给两个人

两次企图　　遇上了两根

不能同时使用的绳子

一个人　　　企图两次使用

一根绳子　　另一个人

企图一次使用两根绳子

他们拉断了绳子

Hu Zi-bo
胡子博 (1972–)

"Relieved" (解脱)

The last piece of ice melted.

I calmly watched it dripping
rubbing my hands together, unable to avoid the sun's
    long nails.

I put on my clothes singing
a pop song, "Who is the kaleidoscope under the sun?"
daylight all over the place, strange temperatures everywhere
hot, extremely hot
He starts to have dreams during the day
often awkwardly bumping into himself running
mad
on the street
In time, he has tied himself with a rope.

Now I curl up in my sleep
toss and turn with worry
ice melts fast in my dreams
rubbing my hands together, rubbing again
rubbing my hands again
my complexion gradually softens.

最后一块冰也化啦　　　我搓搓手
很平静地看着
水一滴一滴往下掉
阳光的指甲长得令人无法回避
我穿上衣服
不停地唱流行歌　　　　"谁是
真正的阳光下的三棱镜"
四处弥漫的极昼　　　遍布异象
天气很热
人们都是在白天做梦
经常在街上 尴尬地碰到
自己在梦中疯跑　　　时间长了
只能用绳子把他系住
现在　　　　我睡觉
还是蜷着身子
我对此深感焦虑
一次次彻夜难眠
睡梦中的冰化得好快
我搓搓手　　我再次搓搓手
我又搓搓手
我让自己的脸色慢慢柔和起来

"Crossroads" (十字街头)

At the crossroads
I could not see where
he emerged.

Was it from the alley to the left
or the horse-drawn carriageway to the right
or out of the post office
or the liquor store next door to the post office
or the market next to the liquor store?

Did he sneak up from behind me
the one who covered my eyes?

I saw him, another "apparition of these faces in the crowd"[16]
but I still could not tell you who he really was.

十字街头
我没看见他
是从哪里出来的
是左边那条小巷?
右边那辆宝马?
还是小巷旁边那个邮局?
邮局旁边那个酒店?
酒店旁边那个商场?
抑或从我的身后
他就是那个
刚刚蒙住我眼睛的人?
我看见他
走在来来往往形形色色的人群中
但我一直没看清
他到底是哪一个人

(2009)

---

16. Ezra Pound. "In a Station of the Metro." *Personae*. (1926).

Xie Xiang-nan
谢湘南 (1974–)

"Report of a Work-related Injury" (一起工伤事故的调查报告)

> Gong Zhong-hui
> Female
> Twenty years old
> Native of Jiangxi province
> ID Number: Z0264
> Department: Molding
> Line of Work: Beer machine
> Employment Date: 24 August 1997
>
> While stocking beer machine,
>   product fails to drop into mold
> Safety door fails to open
> Putting her hand in from the side
> to push product down
> Hand touches
> safety door
> Mold folds
> Crushing hand
> Middle finger and little finger
> Two segments of middle finger, one segment of pinkie
> Result of investigation:
> "Violation of factory safety procedures"
>
> Accordingly
> her hands had been burned often.
> Accordingly
> she had been on the job for over twelve hours.
> After the accident, she

accordingly

did not cry.

neither did she

holler

holding her fingers she

staggered

At the time of the accident
there were no witnesses.

龚忠会
女
20 岁
江西吉安人
工卡号：Z0264
部门：注塑
工种：啤机
入厂时间：970824

啤塑时，产品未落，安全门
未开
从侧面伸手入模内脱
产品。手
触动
安全门
合模时
压烂
中指及无名指
中指2节，无名指一节
调查结果
属"违反工厂　　　安全操作归程"

据说

她的手经常被机器烫出泡

据说

她已连续工作了十二小时

据说事发后 她

没哭　　　也没

喊叫　　　她握着手指

走

事发当时　无人

目　　　睹　　现　　　场

Shu
竖 (1972–)

"Alive" (活着)

A circle
A rectangle
Four right triangles
This is a composite
although
it resembles him
  only
  roughly

He has not bathed for a long time
very dirty
on the side of the composite I write
"filthy..."
He is not bad
On the side I draw
another circle
another rectangle
four right triangles
resembling another person

I want to say they are friends
So
I link his right triangle
with his/her ninety-degree triangle
I draw a line
symbolizing the horizon

symbolizing they are still alive
also
they have lots of time to kill

一个圆
一个矩形
四个纯角三角形
这是一个人的画像
虽然
只有胖瘦像他

他很久没洗过澡了
很脏
我就在旁边写上
脏啊。。。。。。
他不坏
我就在他边上
又画了一个圆
一个矩形
四个纯角三角形
代表另一个人

我想说他们是朋友
所以
我把他的一个纯角三角形
和他(她)的一个纯角三角形连在一块
我还画了一条线
代表地平线
代表他们还活着
并且
有的是时间

Pan Mo-zi
潘漠子 (1972–)

"**Melodrama**" (小悲剧)

1.
Places where birds fly
are named empty space.
Birds first
Then emptiness

2.
Doors, always open
There must also be a door to hell

3.
The sun approves everything

4.
Me, you, he:
A spear, a shield, a blacksmith

5.
Those who say the earth is vast
are those who are constantly hiding

6.
Those full of tears
contain rivers and the sea

7.
Relative to WE
THEY is a word that dies fast

8.

Getting ahead or falling behind
The important thing is to die on the road

9.

Looking at the mountain, it is not a mountain
Looking at the water, it is hard to determine if it is water
Looking at people, they are not people

10.

First believe in the existence of earth
Then look at the cloud

11.

The most beautiful void
is nothing more than the beauty of an empty vase

The biggest void
is nothing more than a heart without earth

1。

有鸟飞过的地方
叫做虚空
先有鸟
后有空虚

2。

门，一直敞开着
一定还有地狱之门

3。

阳光认可一切

4。
我，你，他：
一矛，一盾，一个铁匠

5。
说大地辽阔的人
是无处不在藏身的人

6。
饱含热泪的人
包含大江，大河，大海

7。
相对于我们
他们是死得最快的词语

8。
抢在前面还是落在后面
重要的是死在路上

9。
看山不是山
看水难为水
看人不像人

10。
先相信有土
后抬头看云

11。
最美的空虚
莫过于花瓶里无花

最大的空虚
莫过于心里无土

Mo Tou Bei Bei
魔头贝贝 (1973–)

"Small Pain" (小疼)

Night time trees are vast and dark

I, in the deepest of the night, appear
clutching an empty bottle
flinging the empty bottle
staring, blankly, there

I, under the massive dark trees, appear
very small.
The sound of the breaking bottle
  very pale, very painful, very sharp

I, under the huge and dark trees, flicker
invisible

晚上的树大而黑

我就在那时 出现
拎着空酒瓶
甩掉空酒瓶
我就在那里 瞪眼

在大而黑的树下
我很小
碎的声音很白　很疼　很尖

在大而黑的树下
我火花一闪　　　　没人看见

"Oeuvre 45" (作品45号)

Falling falling, human heads all over
  yet still panning for extrication.
their clumsiness makes me love so embarrassingly hot.
Chaos!
road ahead harbors unknown danger.
Getting over hidden doorway
hide as everyday drinking and eating.

Over another land creation
another bout of violent drinking
human head human head human head me forget me

sure is

an inevitable error

(Composed March 1992 in jail)

落了又落人头天下虽然悲仍遥望解脱。
他们笨拙我爱得尴尬炽热。
乱啊!
道路居心叵测。
登上危险的领袖阴暗
躲
乃日常的壮烈吃喝。

另一片江山必婉转开创
另一场大醉
人头人头人头我我忘我

也是
无奈的错。
1992.3.23.狱中

"Oeuvre 57" (作品57号)

> Floating towards dusk
> reflected in the mirror of a lake
>   empty, bone chilling, searching.
> My eyes shut to contemplate the flowers
> They open to see the petals falling.
> Deeply absorbed in a mindless game.

> 静里的漂泊偏向迟暮。
> 空空的找到看身外刺骨。
> 闭眼花开
> 睁眼花落。
> 太沉的游戏无缘无故。
> 1992.5.3.狱中

"Oeuvre 65" (作品65号)

> Taking a heavy-footed constitution, tears fill my eyes
> Ah, slow-motion explosion,
> Flow.

> Rainy night
> lost
> (Written in jail, 1992)

> 为什么含泪的细节在暮年里揪心散步?
> 啊缓缓的崩溃
> 和流淌

> 夜雨
> 茫茫。
> 1992.6.19.狱中

"Cold Spell" (寒流)

Inserting a knife in its sheath is like putting me back in my
body.
Peaceful on the outside.

There are some who are striving, and some
giving up completely.

Night falls, the sky darkens once more
though night will pass.

I am on guard: I compose poetry.
boundless sky emotes little meaning.

把刀插进刀鞘就象
把我放回肉体里。
表面的平静。

活着的人，有的还在争取，有的
已完全放弃。

夜晚来了。天
又黑了。虽然夜晚终将过去。

我在守卫：我在写诗。
星空辽阔，毫无意义。

(2002/01/26)

"The Metro Station" (车站汇聚了出发和离别)

> The metro conjoins departures and farewells
> Experience, however, is not straight like the rail track.
> I arrive
> no welcome
> familiar places pass by
> unnoticed.

> 车站汇聚了出发和离别
> 但经历
> 不会象笔直的铁轨。
> 当我回来
> 没有迎接
> 熟悉的场景仿佛路过的
> 那些无名之处。

> (2003/02/23)

Shui Jing Zhu Lian
水晶珠链 (1981–)

"Envy" (羡慕)

I spot the boundless
sky, sea, grassland, grazing cows and goats.
They are utterly unrelated to love.
Their boundless and limitless naiveté and healthy appetite
give them no time to bother with heartbreak.

我看到一些无边无际的东西
天空，海洋，草地，吃草的牛羊
它们跟爱一点关系也没有
无边无际的天真与好胃口
让它们顾不上心碎

Duo Yu
朵渔 (1973–)

"Ode to the West Wind" (西风颂)

A little girl in a pair of thinly padded pants clutching a big
yam. Her beautiful, double-lidded eyes catch
not the high-speed wheels
mucus doubles down her nostrils, frozen
in the afternoon quiet.

The little thinly clothed girl figures
   not how many hearts are
in this city, just as she cannot imagine
who her grown beauty would inspire
to chat and laugh
in the café.

Standing in the west wind, like so
plenty happy, let alone it blows Mom's fire
red hot.
A yam roasting country woman, Mom
cannot imagine what the west wind can mean
to her daughter. This cannot be the same as
a few samplings after a winter storm.

Nothing to curse and every life finds its own
happiness. Even against current, the west wind enters
the delicate neck of the little girl, like the hands pulling
on the guillotine,
and those same hands caressing their girls in the field.

穿薄棉裤的小女儿，抱着一只
硕大的红薯。她美丽的双眼皮
跟不上车轮的速度，
两串小鼻涕　　　　　凝固
在午后的寂静中

穿薄棉裤的小女儿，还想象不出
这座城市有几颗心脏，就像
想象不出她日后的美丽
会让谁在咖啡馆
谈笑风生

站在西风里，这样
就已经很幸福，何况西风
将母亲的炉火吹得彤红。
烤红薯的
乡下母亲，她也没想到一场西风对女儿
意味着什么，这肯定不同于
一场风雪之于几株幼树。

没有什么值得诅咒，每一个
生命都找到了自己的
幸福。甚至逆行的西风，它
钻进了小女儿细小的脖颈，这样的作法恰如
脚手架上的民工将菜地里的女友轻抚。。。。。。

The Artists

Cao Fei
曹飞 (1978–)

A native of Guangzhou, Cao Fei is one of the prominent figures on the Beijing art scene. Her work critically examines the new era of cosmopolitan life by subtly depicting subjects on the verge of social and cultural dislocation. *Not Going Home Tonight* and *Beautiful Dog Brows* depict female characters as the subject of newly found sexual freedom, satirizing a society that blindly follows -isms and movements, particularly influences from the West.

Beautiful Dog Brows, 2001. Photograph (courtesy of Cao Fei @ Fresh Series 2002 and www.caofei.com).

Not Going Home Tonight, 2002. Photograph (courtesy of Cao Fei @ Fresh Series 2002 and www.caofei.com).

Zhang Da-li
张大力 (1963-)

Zhang Da-li is well known in Beijing for his trademark silhouettes of human heads sprayed on abandoned buildings. Like other visual artists who devoted a period of their studio practice to the subject of the transformation of the Chinese landscape, Zhang exposes the costs of the seemingly unstoppable drive toward modernization, the market economy, and industrialization.

Demolition: World Financial Center, Beijing,1998. Chromogenic print (collection of China National Art Gallery; images courtesy of the artist and 367Art, Inc. -367艺术网, Beijing).

Demolition: Forbidden City, Beijing, 1998. Chromogenic print (courtesy of the artist and CourtYard Gallery, Beijing).

Dialogue, 1996.
Chromogenic
print. (collection
of China National
Art Gallery;
image courtesy of
the artist and
CourtYard Gallery,
Beijing).

Leong Sze-tsung
梁思聪 (1970-)

Like Zhang Da-li's subject matter, the work of Leong Sze-Tsung examines the spatial consequences of rapid urban development in China. The photographs record the instantaneous disappearance of "old" China and appearance of the "new," a process that in some cases wipes out entire cities for new development. Leong records precise moments in the history of such historic places as the Xuanwu District of Beijing, where Ming and Qing dynasty courtyard houses, partially destroyed, wait to be demolished to make way for luxury housing; or a field of rubble that is now Old Fengdu, a city razed to make way for the Three Gorges Dam. Leong captures the physical implications of this development process—landscapes imprinted with both irrevocable loss and anticipation of the future.

Old Fengdu, Chongqing Municipality, 2002. Photograph (courtesy of International Center of Photography and the Asia Society, New York).

No. 6 Huashishang Fourth Lane, Chongwen District, Beijing, 2003. Photograph (courtesy of International Center of Photography and the Asia Society, New York).

The scale of urban development currently underway in China is by far the greatest in the world, and yet these photographs are not only about China. As Leong says, "They are about urban erasure, historical absence, and new development of which China may currently have some of the clearest and perhaps most extreme manifestations." Though the physical outcome of these development projects may be familiar, it remains to be seen how the widespread loss of cultural heritage in built form will affect the future of these cities, and others like them all over the world.

Sheng Qi
盛奇 (1965–)

Sheng Qi's *Memories (Me)* uses a photographic portrait of the artist as a little boy nesting in the hand of a presumably hard-working man or woman whose missing finger is likely the result of a work-related accident. It is the perfect visual accompaniment to two of the most poignant and powerful works in this volume, Xie Xiang-nan's "Report of a Work-related Injury" and Liu Chun's "Purity." Industrialization has a double edge. It accomplishes wonders in terms of improving "lifestyle" by such quantitative measures as "living standards." Yet the damage to the hand shows us the price of a vastly enhanced income is a disability. Somehow, apart from all this, the child in the picture remains unchanged. The artist does not wish to grow older and have to grapple with a changing society. Like Dorian Gray in reverse, he does age but wishes to remain innocent in the sense of William Blake's "Songs of Innocence." His identity involuntarily faces a crisis. In fact, the artist cut his own finger off, and this is his hand as well as self-portrait.

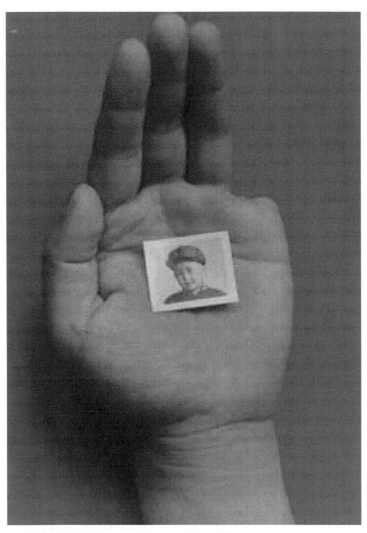

Memories (Me), 2000. Photograph (courtesy of the artist).

Biographical Sketches

The Poets

Hai Zi (海子, 1964–89) was born in Anhui province with the given name Zha Hai-sheng. Admitted to Beijing University's law program at fifteen, under the *nom de plume* of Hai Zi he started writing poetry during his junior year. While a professor of philosophy and aesthetics at People's University in Beijing, Hai Zi self-published his poetry collections *Danshi Shui, Shui* (但是水，水; *But Water, Water*), Tudi (土地; *Earth*), and poetry drama *Taiyang* (太阳; *The Sun*). In 1988, Hai Zi finished the first volume of his poetry drama trilogy, *Assassin* (刺客). Upon the request of his fans, many of them college students, Hai Zi would end his lectures by reciting his most recent poems. On March 26, 1989, Hai Zi ended his life at age twenty-five, leaving behind two million words of poetry, drama, fiction, and essays. "Overlooking the Ocean" was posthumously anthologized in Chinese high school textbooks nationwide.

Ge Mai (戈麦, 1967–91) was born on a farm in Heilongjiang province on the northeast border of China with the given name of Zhu Fu-jun. A good friend of Hai Zi's, Ge followed suit and ended his life in 1991 by drowning in Wanquan River in the western suburbs of Beijing. Ge Mai entered Beijing University and majored in Chinese Language and Literature. Upon graduation in 1989, Ge was assigned to the editorial team of the *Zhongguo Wenxuei* (中国文学; *China Literary Journal*). In his brief poetic career spanning 1985 to his untimely death, Ge was a prolific writer, leaving behind volumes of poetry and essays. In one essay, Ge stated, "Poetry should be language's sharp ax; it splits open soul's frozen river...; it directly relates to the imaginary mind, creates an open space between mind and body, and makes possible the impossible."

Xiao An (小安, 1964–) resides in Chengdu, the capital of Sichuan province and an historic literary city made famous by Du Fu in the Tang dynasty. A Dada figure in the 1980s, her major works include *Zhong Yanye de Nuren* (种烟叶的女; *The Female Tobacco Planter*), *Zhizhu Yi* (蜘蛛一; *Spider 1*), *Lushang Yizhan Deng* (路上一盏灯; *A Light on the Road*), *Women Laixie Shi* (我们来写诗; *Let's Write Poetry*), *Neixin Shijie* (内心世界; *Inner World*), and *Fuqi Shenghuo* (夫妻生活; *Life Between a Husband and Wife*). "There was a time when my days were spent in loneliness; only for writing poetry. But my work during that time does not reflect my sorrows and solitude. I calmly dealt with my feelings. I think that my poems are happy and beautiful occurrences," she comments.

Yin Li-chuan (尹丽川, 1973–) was born in Chongqing and resides in Beijing. Educated at Beijing University with a degree in Western languages and literature, Yin later entered the French ESEC school specializing in film production. A participant in the "Lower Body" poetry movement, Yin's poems address China's modern-day family values and parent-child relationships. They exhibit a feminine sensitivity in their linguistic diction and convey a sure reassessment of the traditional Chinese family values. Since her debut as a poet in 1999, Yin has published a poetry collection *Zai Shufu Yixie* (再舒服一些; *Got to Be More Comfortable*) and a novel, *Jianren* (贱人; *The Cheap Bastard*). On top of her popularity as a female poet, Yin has recently entered the male-dominated film industry. Her latest films include her debut *Gongyuan* (公园; *Park*), which was short-listed at the Moscow International Film Festival.

Tan Ke-xiu (谭克修, 1971–) was born in Hunan province and serves on the editorial committee of the journal, *Hunan City Planning*. He graduated from Xi'an Science and Architecture University and is the chief architect of Hunan's Fangyuan Architectural and Engineering firm. In the late 1980s, Tan began writing poetry during his leisure time. Tan was a winner at China's annual poetry contest and his published poems include *Luoxiang Xi'an de Xue* (落向西安的雪; *Snow Falling Toward Xi'an*), *Mou Xiancheng Guihua* (某县城规划; *A Certain County Planning*), *Hainan Liuri You* (海南六日游; *Six Days in Hainan*), and *Huanxiang Riji* (还乡日记; *Home Coming Diaries*). In 2003, Tan launched the literary journal *Mingtian* (公园; *Tomorrow*).

Yu Xiang (宇向, 1970–) was born and lives in Jinan, Shandong province. She won first place in the eleventh annual poetry contest of China's *Poetry Monthly* journal. Extolled by critics for displaying a poetic style similar to that of Elizabeth Bishop, Yu's diction is at once carefree and crafted, natural and forceful. "Poetic expression is a sudden impulse and yet it is natural to me as well. Perhaps they are two magic forces like magnets attracted to each other: poetry and I, especially when my poetry occurs at a peaceful time in life. It allows me to reflect on my wasted days and precious moments, examining a chain of internal conflicts. I do not use too many words. I talk very little and confine my expression to what comes naturally."

Liu Chun (刘春, 1970–) was born in a small village in Guangxi province and now resides in Guilin. His poems have appeared in numerous literary journals and magazines including *Renmin Wenxue* (人民文学; *People Literature*), *Qingnian Wenxue* (青年文学; *Youth Literature*), *Shige Pinglun* (诗歌评论; *Poetry Review*), *Beijing Wenxue* (北京文学; *Beijing Literature*), and *Nanfang Luntan* (南方论坛; *Southern Forum*). His honors include the Guangxi government's Drum Award and World Wide Web Best Poetry Award. Liu Chun is author of three poetry collections, *Youshang de Yueliang* (忧伤的月亮; *Melancholy Moon*), *Yuncaoche Chuanguo Chengshi* (运草车穿过城; *The Hay Carrying Cart Passing through the City*), and *Guangxi Dangdai Zuojia Congshu* (广西当代作家丛书; *Guangxi Contemporary Writers' Chronicle*).

Zhu Qing-he (朱庆和, 1973–) was born in Shandong province and graduated from Southeast University in Nanjing. He started composing poetry in 1998 and has published a collection titled *Criss-Cross Run, Love Mechanics*. Zhu also launched a popular magazine, *Zhongjian* (中间; *In Between*). Zhu resides in Nanjing.

Hu Xu-dong (胡续东, 1974–) was born in the small village of Hechuan in the northern part of Chongqing and entered Beijing University's Chinese Literature department in 1996. Hu received his Ph.D. in 2002 and is an associate professor of literature at the World Literature Research Institute at Beijing University. Hu lectured in Brazil from 2003 to 2005 and is author of three collections of poetry, *Shuide Bianyuan* (水的边缘; *From the Water's Edge*), *Fengnai* (风奶; *Wind Milk*), and *Ai Shi Liugan* (爱是流感; *When Love is a Spreading Disease*). Hu's poetry career started in

1992 and some of his poetry has been translated into English, Spanish, German, Flemish, Japanese, French, Swedish, and Portuguese. Hu was awarded many prizes including the *Liu Li-An* and *Tomorrow* poetry honors.

Jiang Fei (江非, 1974–) was born in Shandong

province. In 2008, Jiang moved to Hainan island and worked as an editor for literary journals. His most recent publication, a 2009 collection of 108 poems entitled *Dujiao Xi* (独角戏; *Solo Drama*) won wide acclaim in China. His previous major publications include *Yizhi Mayi Shanglu le* (一只蚂蚁上路了; *An Ant Is on the Go*) and *Jinian Ce* (纪念册; *Memorabilia*) published respectively by The Writers Publishing House in 2004 and Hai Feng Publishing House in 2007.

Yang Chun-min (杨春民, 1979–) was born

Gu-shi (固始), in Henan province. He received a BA in 2002 from the Communication University of China in Beijing and went on to take an MA from China's Central University of Finance and Economics.

Shi Yi-long (石一龙, 1976–) born with the

given name of Shi Long in Anhui province. Shi graduated from Nanjing University with a degree in Chinese literature and is a newsman at CCTV. A member of the Chinese Writers Association, Shi has published the poetry collections *Zhuifeng Shaonian* (追风少年; *Wind-Chasing Youth*), *Bu Cunzai de Yiwang* (不存在的遗忘; *Absent Amnesia*), *Xinglu Cangmang* (行旅苍茫; *Ceaseless Journey*), and essays in journals.

Ma Fei (马非, 1971–) was born in Liaoning province with the given name of Wang Shao-yu, Ma was admitted into the Chinese Language and Literature program at Shanxi Teacher's College and graduated in 1993. He has been working at Qinghai People's Publishing House since then. Ma's poetry has been published in numerous collections and his solo poetry collection *Mafei Shixuan 2000–2006* (马非诗选 2000–2006; *Ma Fei Poetry Collection 2000–2006*) was published by Qinghai People's Press in 2007.

Huang Jin-ming (黄金明, 1974–) born in Guangdong province. After graduating from Guangdong Institute of Education in 1998, Huang went to work at Nanfang Daily Press Group. Huang's poetry and essays have appeared in numerous literary journals in China and his poetry collection *Dalu Chaotian* (大路朝天; *Heading Into Thin Air*) was published by Beijing Relay Press in 1997. He resides in Guangzhou.

Sheng Xing (盛兴, 1978–) was born and lives in Linyi city, Shandong province. Sheng Xing's poetry takes on a conservative form with yet a progressive radical content. Sheng uses seemingly "soft" language to emote a sharp criticism of social and political ills. Sheng participated in the poetry movement called Xiabanshen (下半身; Lower Body) in 2000 and his poetry and fiction have been published in People's Literary Journal, *Dajia* (大家; *Everyone*), *Furong* (芙蓉; *The Peony Review*), and *Tianya* (天涯; *Earth's End*).

Song Lie-yi (宋烈毅, 1973–) lives in Anhui province. His works have appeared in *Shikan* (诗刊; *Poetry Review*), *Shige Yuekan* (诗歌月刊; *Poetry Monthly*), *Xiandai Shi* (现代诗; *Modern Poetry*) and other journals in China. Song received the top prize at the Hong Kong's 30th Youth Literature Award.

Hu Zi-bo (胡子博, 1972–) was born in a small village in Shandong province and now resides in Guilin. Hu participated in the planning and publication of *Xiandai Shijing* (现代诗经; *Contemporary Poetry*) edited by Yi Sha and published by Lijiang Publishers in 2004–2005. Hu's recent publications include *Shimianzhe* (失眠者; *Insomnia*), *Qihou* (气候; *Weather*), *Jietuo* (解脱; *Relieved*), *Xushi* (叙事; *Reminiscence*), *Shijie* (世界; *Universe*), and *Bukezhi de Shi* (不可知的事; *The Unkown*).

Xie Xiang-nan (谢湘南, 1974–) was born in Hunan province and resides in the special economic zone of Shenzhen. After dropping out of high school in 1992, Xie worked odd jobs in construction and security. In 1993, Xie started writing poetry, and has since published hundreds of poems in journals, anthologies, and solo volumes. His poetry collection *Lingdian de Banyungong* (零点的搬运工; *Midnight Movers*) was published in 2000.

Pan Mo-zi (潘漠子, 1972–) was born in Anhui province. With a BA in fine art from Anhui Teachers College in 1996, Pan moved to Shengzhen to start his own business, Cangsang Culture and Art Limited. Pan wrote poetry while working as an art consultant and in 2000 published his epic poem, "Needs" in the journal *Everyone*. Later works have since been published in various poetry journals including "Flower City" and "South" in *Poetry Review*. Pan views contemporary life in China as a matter of material wealth without depth: "The world we live in today contains too much material sediments and our souls are distorted. Permeating all is the smell of material gain. We have lost the wealth of generations past. My grandpa was an architect. He carried with him our traditional cultural virtues. He would take his son's door down to build his neighbor's house. Our generation has lost those virtues. We have also lost a sense of responsibility. Our generation no longer appreciates reading and my creation is not met with equal minds." Pan now lives in Beijing.

Shu (竖, 1972–) was born in Shanghai and resides in Beijing. No picture of the poet is available.

MoTou BeiBei (魔头贝贝, 1973–) was born in Henan province and resides in Anyang. Once jailed as a dissident, Mo Tou Bei Bei now works in an oil refinery supply company in Anyang. The internet identity he chose represents an oxymoron combining *motou* (bloody and violent) and *beibei* (darling and cherubic).

Shui Jing Zhu Lian (水晶珠链, 1981–) was born in Handan, Hebei province with the given the name of Chen Huan. At age 16, still in high-school, Chen achieved nationwide recognition for her internet-disseminated fiction, and soon gained an even wider reputation with the publication of her first novel, *Kuqi de Wutong* (哭泣的梧桐; *The Weeping Tung Tree*), but not before much trial and tribulation. Just on the verge of its publication as part of a series for young readers, the novel was withdrawn by the publishers on the grounds that its content could have been considered "unsuitable" (the book includes an account of a love affair between a teacher and a student). It was later published by the prestigious Writers Press. She has also published her more recent, and acclaimed, collection of poetry and essays, *Pianyao Zuomeinu* (偏要作美女; *Just Gotta Be Gorgeous*).

Duo Yu (朵渔, 1973–) was born in Shandong province with the given name of Gao Zhao-liang. In 1994 he graduated from Beijing Teachers College with a BA in Chinese literature. In 2000, Duo Yu started the Xia Banshen (下半身; Lower Body) poetry movement and has since published poetry collections, *Anjie* (暗街; *Dark Street*), *Gaoyuanshang* (高原上; *Highland*) and *Feichangai* (非常爱; *Bountiful Love*). Duo Yu is now editor-in-chief of the journal *Shikan Xianchang* (诗歌现场; *Poetry Scene*), and lives in Tianjin.

The Artists

Cao Fei (曹飞, 1978–) was born in Guangzhou and works and resides in Beijing. She graduated from Guangzhou Academy in 2001. Cao's video and photography have been exhibited throughout Asia and the West. Her exhibitions include "Past in Reverse: Contemporary Art of East Asia" in 2006 at the Hood Museum of Art, Dartmouth College, the third stop of a touring group exhibition that was inaugurated by the San Diego Museum of Art in 2005; "Between Past and Future: New Photography and Video from China" in 2004 at the International Center of Photography and the Asia Society and Museum in New York; and the 50th Venice Biennale in 2003. Cao was Artist in Residence at the invitation of Robert Wilson at the Water Mill Art Center in summer, 2004.

Zhang Da-li (张大力, 1963–) was born in Harbin, Heilongjiang province, and graduated from National Academy of Fine Arts and Design in Beijing in 1987. His exhibitions include "Beijing in London" at Institute of Contemporary Art, London; "Group Exhibition" at Mu Art Foundation, Eindhoven, "Contemporary Chinese Art, Literature and Culture" at Bard College, New York; "Group Exhibition" at Cypress College and BC Space Gallery Cypress, CA; "Chinese Contemporary" in London; and the performance "The World Is Yours" at the Design Museum, Beijing. In 1993 and 1994, he had solo shows at Peter Dunsch Gallerie, Essen, Germany and Galleria Studio 5, Bologna, Italy.

Leong Sze-tsung (梁思聪, 1970–) was born in Mexico City and currently lives and works in New York. His solo exhibitions include "History Images" at Yossi Milo Gallery, New York, 2006, and "History Images" at the Storefront for Art and Architecture, New York, 2004. Group exhibitions include "New Photography: Photographs by Taryn Simon, Sze Tsung Leong, Ruth Dusseault, and Angela West" at the High Museum of Art, Atlanta, 2006; "Landscape: Recent Acquisitions at The Museum of Modern Art," New York, 2006; IX Biennale de La Habana: Dynamics of Urban Culture, Centro de Arte Contemporáneo Wifredo Lam, Havana, Cuba, 2006; "Beyond Delirious: Architecture in Selected Photographs from the Ella Fontanals Cisneros Collection," Cisneros Fontanals Art Foundation, Miami, 2005; "Convergence at E116/N40, Beijing" 798 Dayaolu Workshop, Beijing, 2005; "Celebrating Twenty Years: Gifts in Honor of the Hood Museum of Art," Hood Museum of Art, Dartmouth College, 2005; "The City: Contemporary Views of the Built Environment," Lehman College Art Gallery/CUNY, New York, 2005; "Between Past and Future: New Photography and Video From China," International Center for Photography, New York, 2004; "Est-Ouest/Nord-Sud," Arc en Rêve, Bordeaux, 2004; and "Painting as Paradoxa," at Artists Space, New York, 2002, curated by Lauri Firstenburg. Leong's art is part of the permanent collection of The Museum of Modern Art, New York; San Francisco Museum of Modern Art; High Museum of Art, Atlanta; International Center of Photography, New York; Brooklyn Museum of Art; Santa Barbara Museum of Art; University of Chicago, Davis Museum; and Cultural Center, Wellesley College; Hood Museum of Art, Dartmouth College; and Cisneros Fontanals Art Foundation, Miami. In 2005, Leong received a John Simon Guggenheim Memorial Foundation Fellowship and a New York State Council on the Arts Grant.

Sheng Qi (盛奇, 1965–) was born in Hefei, Anhui province. He graduated with an MFA from Central Saint Martin's College of Art and Design, London. Sheng Qi lives and works in Beijing. His selected solo exhibitions include "Transcribe," Red Gate Gallery, Beijing, 2003; "Video Installation," Melbourne Fringe Festival, Mass Gallery, Melbourne, 2000; "Are You Willing to Shake My Hand?," Tokyo, "Nine Pigeons + Sheng Qi," Beijing, and "Handicapped Man," Beijing, 1999; "Fortune Cookies," Institute of Contemporary Art, London, 1997. The artist is better known for severing his pinky from his left hand in 1989 and leaving for Europe shortly after. As a founding member of Concept 21, a Chinese performance art group in the 1980s, Sheng Qi continued to use performance art as well as painting with ink and blood to rally against the ignorance of social problems in China.

At F2 Gallery in Beijing in August 2009, the artist presented five different series of works that he had developed concurrently over the previous three years. The canvases were dripping with paint as a number of pressing social issues were examined in Shenq Qi's intentionally messy way. "Power of the People" in August of 2009 celebrated the Chinese people who constitute the subjects and major actors of Sheng Qi's dramatic imagination. The show also highlighted the artist's objective to present the world around him as it really appeared to him—a profoundly beautiful chaos—as if to say that clear vision was the first step to both personal and artistic freedom.

The Translators

Keming Liu (刘克明) is an associate professor of English at Medgar Evers College of the City University of New York, where she teaches literature, linguistics, and composition. She is also a guest lecturer at Long Island University's C.W. Post campus, where she teaches Chinese literature and the arts. Aside from publications in scholarly journals on language and literature, Liu is a board member of the American Society of Geolinguistics. In 1987, her translation of Henry James's "Hugh Merrow" was published in the literary journal of Shanghai's East China Normal University. Selected translations from this anthology appeared in *Natural Bridge* and *Seneca Review*. Liu holds a doctorate in linguistics from Columbia University's Teachers College. A native of Boading, Hebei province, she resides in New York City and Cutchogue, Long Island.

Joanna Sit (薛观华) is a lecturer in the English department at Medgar Evers College of the City University of New York. She holds an MFA from Brooklyn College and her poems have appeared in *Poetry Motel, California Review, The Relief Journal, Tonopah Review, Fickle Muses,* and other literary journals. Her long poem "Bitten by an Unusual Fly" was included in the anthology *Monologues From The Road,* published by Heinemann Press. She has read at the Knitting Factory, Teachers and Writers Collaborative, Dixon Place, La Mama La Galleria, the 11th Street Bar, Cornelia Street Cafe, and Asian American Asian Research Institute. Poems she translated for this anthology appeared in *Natural Bridge* and *Seneca Review*. She also read passages in Chinese for the multilingual reading of Allen Ginsberg's poem "Howl." She resides in Brooklyn, New York.

Yuan Jia-li (院佳莉) teaches English as a Foreign Language at Hebei University of Science and Technology, and was in Australia for research as a visiting scholar in 2007. Yuan graduated with a BA in English from Hebei Teachers University in 1982 and has published scholarly articles in various journals in China. These include "Teaching and Learning; English Writing of College Students" (2002), "Wuthering Heights: Heathcliff, the Revengeful Character" (2002), both in *Literature Studies*, and "Language Behavior and Social Culture" (2002), in *Chinese Higher Education Study*. Yuan lives in Shijiazhuang, Hebei province, China.

Zhao Jian-xun (赵建勋) teaches Chinese language and literature at University of Fukui, Japan. He taught at Beijing Foreign Studies University from 1987 to 1994. Zhao is a prolific writer and translator, whose *Foreign Poetry Masterpiece Guidebook* was published in 1994. Zhao has translated over ten novels from Japanese to Chinese of such writers as Arata Tendo, Hideo Yokoyama, Shogo Utano, Taku Ashibe, Yusuke Kishi, Masako Bandou, and Soji Shimada. In 2008, Zhao translated Yu Dan's "*Notes on Zhuangzi*" (*Zhuang-zi Xinde*) into Japanese ("*Sousi no Kokoro*," Kofuku-no-Kagaku, IRH Press, Japan). Zhao resides in Tsuga City, Fukui Prefecture, Japan.

James Zhao (赵毅) holds a Ph.D. and MA in literary theory from the Department of Chinese Language and Literature at People's University of China in Beijing, and a BA in English language and literature from Hebei Teachers University. Currently he is on the faculty of Beijing Technology and Business University. He was a research fellow on the committee for the Olympic Games Global Impact, commissioned by the IOC and BOCOG. His publications in the fields of linguistics, literary theory, marketing, and philosophy have appeared in various academic journals in China. He served as the deputy editor-in-chief on the team of lexicographers for a Chinese-English dictionary published in 1994 by the Beijing University Press. Zhao has translated many articles and two books from English into Chinese. He acted as Professor J. Hillis Miller's interpreter during his visit to Beijing in June, 2004. Zhao resides in Beijing.

Bibliography

Ashbery, John. *And the Stars Were Shining*. New York: Farrar, Straus, Giroux, 1994.

——. A Worldly Country: New Poems. New York: HarperCollins, 2007.

Auden , W. H. "Sonnets from China, XIII." *W. H. Auden Collected Poems*. Ed. Edward
Mendelson. New York: Random House, 1976: 154.

Auster, Paul Benjamin. *The Brooklyn Follies*. New York: Henry Holt and Company-
Macmillan, 2005.

Auster, Paul Benjamin, ed. *The Random House Book of Twentieth Century French Poetry*.
New York: Vintage-Random House, 1984.

Bernstein, Richard. "The Panda Roared." *The New York Times, Week in Review*,
20 July 2008.

Eliot , T. S. "Four Quartets." *The Complete Poems and Plays of T. S. Eliot 1909–1950*.
New York: Harcourt, Brace & World, 1971: 115–122.

Ge Mai. *Gemai Shi Quanpian* (戈麦诗全编; *The Complete Poetic Works of Ge Mai*).
Ed. Xi Du. Shanghai: SDX Joint Publishing Company, 1999.

Goodman, D.S.G. *Beijing Street Voices*. London: Marion Boyars Publishers, 1981.

Hogan, Patrick. "Literary Universals and Their Cultural Traditions: The Case of
Poetic Imagery." *Consciousness, Literature and the Arts* 6.2 (August 2005):
Special Issue: Literary Universals. March 2007.

Hai Zi. *Tudi* (土地; *Earth*). Liaoning: Chunfeng Literature and Art Publishing House, 1990.

Hong, Zi-cheng and Deng-han Liu. *Zhongguo Dangdai Xinshi Shi* (中国当代新诗; *History
of Contemporary Chinese Poetry*). Beijing: Peking University Press, 2005.

Huang, Jin-ming. *Dalu Chaotian* (大 路 朝 天; *Heading Into Thin Air*). Beijing:
Relay Press, 1997.

Jia, Wensha. *The Remaking of the Chinese Character and Identity in the 21st Century*.
Westport, CT: Praeger Publishers, 2001.

Jiang Fei. *Dujiao Xi* (独角戏; *Solo Drama: Collection of 108 Jiang Fei Recent Poems*). Haikou,
China: South China Press, 2009.

Larkin, Philip. "Philip Larkin Praises the Poetry of Thomas Hardy." *The Listener* 25,
July 1968: 111.

Li, Xue-qin. *Eastern Zhou and Qin Civilization*. Trans. Chang, K.C. New Haven, CT: Yale University Press, 1985.

Ma, Fei. *Mafei Shixuan* (马 非 诗 选 2000-2006; *Ma Fei Poetry Collection 2000–2006*). Qinghai, China: Qinghai People's Press, 2007.

Pound, Ezra. *Personae: Collected Short Poems*. New York: New Directions, 1971.

San Diego Museum of Art. *Past in reverse: Contemporary Art of East Asia*. California: San Diego Museum of Art, 2004.

San Francisco Museum of Modern Art. *Half-Life of a Dream: Contemporary Chinese Art from the Logan Collection*. San Francisco: University of San Francisco Press, 2008.

Sansom, Anna. "The Beauty of Progress: Edward Burtynsky's Widescreen Industrial Visions." *Spoon: The Taste of Contemporary Culture*. November/December 2005: 58–65.

Shih, Shu-mei. *Visuality and Identity: Sinophone Articulations Across the Pacific*. Los Angeles, California: University of California Press, 2007.

Tan, Ke-xiu, ed. *Mingtian* (明天; *Tomorrow*). Hunan: Hunan Literature and Art Publishing House, 2003.

Wei, Jennifer M. *Language Choice and Identity Politics in Taiwan*. New York: Lexington Books, 2008.

Yang, Xiao-min, ed. *Zhong-guo Dang-dai Qing-nian Shi-ren Shi-xuan* (中国当代青年诗人诗选; *Selected Poems of Contemporary Chinese Poets*). Shijiazhuang: Hebei Educational Press, 2004.

Yeh , Michelle. "The 'Cult of Poetry' in Contemporary China." *The Journal of Asian Studies* 55.1 (February 1996): 51–80.

Yi, Sha, ed. *Xiandai Shijing* (现代诗经; *Contemporary Poetry*). Guilin, China: Lijiang Publishers, 2004–2005.

Yin, Li-chuan. *Zai Shufu Yixie* (再舒服一些; *Got to Be More Comfortable*). Taiwan: Aquarius Press, 2003.

—— *Jianren* (贱人; *The Cheap Bastard*). Haikou, Hainan: Hainan Press, 2002.

Zhang, Ji. *Cloud Gate Song: The Verse of Tang Poet Zhang Ji*. Trans. Jonathan Chaves. Warren, CT: Floating World Editions, 2006.

Index of Poems